AF668126

LORD KRISHNA
IN THE
BOARDROOM

LORD KRISHNA
IN THE BOARDROOM

B.S. Tirtha Maharaja

newstech
publishing inc

Publishing Coordination:
Newstech Publishing Inc.
www.newstechglobal.com

KONARK

Konark Publishers Pvt Ltd
New Delhi • Seattle

Konark Publishers Pvt. Ltd
206, First Floor,
Peacock Lane, Shahpur Jat,
New Delhi110 049
Phone: +91-11-41055065, 65254972
e-mail: india@konarkpublishers.com
website: www.konarkpublishers.com

Konark Publishers International
8615, 13th Ave SW,
Seattle WA 98106
Phone: (415) 409-9988
e-mail: us@konarkpublishers.com

Copyright © B.S. Tirtha Maharaja, 2015
Illustrations by Amit Kumar, Octopus Inc; www.octopusinc.in

All rights reserved. No part of this book may be reproduced or utilised in any form or by any means, electronic or mechanical, including photocopying, recording, or by any information storage and retrieval system, without prior permission in writing from the publishers.

Cataloging in Publication Data--DK
Courtesy: D.K. Agencies (P) Ltd. <docinfo@dkagencies.com>

B. S. Tirtha Maharaj, *Swami*, 1942- **author**.
Lord Krishna in the boardroom / B.S. Tirtha Maharaja.
pages cm
Includes bibliographical references.

ISBN 9789322008680

1. Krishna (Hindu deity) 2. Boards of directors. 3. Strategic planning. 4. Industrial management. 5. Mahābhārata--Criticism, interpretation, etc. 6. Bhagavadgītā--Criticism, interpretation, etc. I. Title.

DDC 658.422 23

Typeset by Saanvi Graphics, Noida

Printed and bound at Thomson Press (India) Ltd.

Dedication

The Supreme Lord Krishna

The Ultimate Truth, is the Supreme Personality of Godhead, the only one with the total of 64 attributes of the Manifestation of The Supreme and He excels in everything. All potencies – Spiritual, Material and Marginal – are, at the same time, onc with and also different from Lord Krishna. Living beings can relate to Lord Krishna as His servants, friends, parents or conjugal lovers.

Sri Chaitanya Mahaprabhu

The Supreme Lord Krishna in golden complexion, who appeared in Bengal about 500 years ago. He established, preached and promoted the Vaishnava philosophy of total devotion and 'Love of God' by chanting the holy names of Lord Krishna in 'Sankirtan'. Truth and love of God, the highest goal of human life, is the core of his philosophy.

His Divine Grace Bhaktisiddhanta Saraswati Goswami Thakura Praphupad

The most illustrious son of Bhaktivinod Thakura, a realised soul who practised and preached the Gaudiya Vaishnava tradition. He was known as the 'Simha' or Lion Guru among spiritual masters because he taught and trained thousands of his disciples in this transcendental science. He founded 64 Gaudiya centres.

His Divine Grace Bhaktivedenta Shrila Praphupad

Appeared in 1896 in Kolkata, India. He first met his guru, Bhaktisiddhanta Saraswati Goswami Thakura Praphupad, in 1922 who inspired him to devote his life to teaching Vedic knowledge in English.

In 1933, he became his disciple. In 1965, he arrived almost penniless in USA to spread his message and founded the International Society for Krishna Consciousness that grew into a global entity with over a hundred centres before he left his body.

His Divine Grace Bhakti Srirup Bhagavat Goswami Maharaj

A disciple of His Divine Grace Bhaktisiddhanta Saraswati Goswami Thakura Praphupad, he was a great spiritual master, appeared in what is now Bangladesh in 1906. He studied diligently and received a Bachelor of Arts degree and devoted his life to preaching the Vaishnava philosophy through his discourses and Sankirtans right up to a very advanced age.

Contents

Preface ix

Editor's Note xiii

Wisdom: From Oral to Written and Again to Oral xiii

Mahabharata: The Greatest of All The Epics xv

Mahabharata's Main Characters xix

War Strategy xxiv

The Bhagavat Gita xxvii

Your Masterplan from God Himself xxvii

Who is Qualified to Comment on Gita? xxxv

Does the Gita Promote Violence? xxxviii

Comments on the Gita and the Supreme Lord Krishna xli

Shrimad Bhagavatam: The First Encyclopaedia xlv

1 The Centre of All Businesses 1

2 The Mysterious Success Factor 15

3 Ideal Chief Executive 28

4 Ideal Heads of Departments 45

5 Modern Management Techniques 59

6 Managing and Surviving Recession 74

7 Successful Executives Use It or Lose It 90

8 The Ultimate Management Guru 104

Appendix: Karma Capitalism 130

9 Harish, Harry, Hurry, Hari 140

Notes and References 156

Author's Profile: From Sales Executive To Sanyasi 160

Editor's Profile: Kul Bhushan 167

Love God, Not Fear Him 169

GVA Philosophy 171

GVA Way of Life 173

Gaudiya Vaishnava Tradition 175

GVA Global Contacts 177

Preface

Ancient Wisdom for Modern Management

- *I can't stand all this tension, how can I cope with it?*
- *Where can I get mental peace?*
- *Why can't I get along with my family and my colleagues?*
- *What can I do to kick the habits of drinking and smoking?*
- *When will I be financially secure?*

These questions come up regularly when I talk to people in Britain, United States, India or any other country I visit. The same questions are asked after my discourses or during my radio and TV interviews. Everyone faces these basic problems today. Whether young or old, living in the East or West, everyone is looking for answers. The answers are in managing one's life. All of us are managing or trying to manage our lives based on our education, understanding and experience. Unfortunately, all these dimensions are limited in our lives, while the stress of coping with huge and new challenges seems never ending. Whether one is managing a big company, providing a service or running a home, we are all managing our affairs and our lives. So who can be our best management guru? Based on ancient wisdom for modern management, this is the question that has been answered in this book. The management principles that apply to running a modern corporation with hundreds of employees and millions in turnover also apply to running a small enterprise, a consultancy or even a home.

These problems in the corporate sector and in our personal lives are caused by losing our faith in basic values of life; our utter materialistic outlook to satisfy our ego, ease and luxuries; the lack of our self-discipline and self-control; and, above all, excessive greed that shows in our unlimited desires, ugly display of money, cravings and ambitions. So what is the solution? The short and simple solution is to surrender totally to the Supreme Lord Krishna and let Him manage your affairs. Why? Because the Supreme Lord proved beyond all doubt by revealing his '*virat roop*' or 'universal form' in which the entire universe is contained within Him. The Supreme Lord informs Arjuna that placing Himself as a super-soul inside the heart of every living being, He closely supervises their functions, desires and the thought process.

But how does he start? Simple, start chanting the Mahamantra:

Hare Krishna Hare Krishna, Krishna Krishna Hare Hare,
Hare Rama Hare Rama, Rama Rama Hare Hare.

If you want to learn about managing your personal affairs, start reading from Chapter Six to Chapter Nine; for managing corporate affairs, start with Chapter One to Chapter Five. The core message is the same: Surrender to the Supreme Lord Krishna! Only when firmly standing on the Krishna Consciousness platform, a person performing any activity in this world can ultimately become liberated and go back to Godhead.

I am very grateful to Shri Kul Bhushan, an experienced business editor and author, for proposing and successfully completing this publishing project. His enthusiasm never diminished in improving this volume. *Hare Krishna!*

– *B.S. Tirtha Maharaja*, 2015.

Editor's Note

Wisdom: From Oral to Written and Again to Oral

The most popular books that have survived for hundreds, indeed thousands, of years are the ones that were never written down. These books were spoken, learnt by heart and recited from generations to generations. At some stage, they were written by hand for a very few persons but for all others, they were spoken, quoted or recited by word of mouth. These are the books we know today as the Vedas, the Upanishads, the Bhagavat Gita, the Bible, the Quran and the Talmud, among other scriptures.

Originally, scholarship was oral. With the recent advances in information technology, it is again possible to benefit from oral scholarship with voice recordings on the radio, TV and Internet. This approach has been partly followed in this book. Since Shrila Tirtha Maharaj is constantly travelling and interacting with people across many continents, it is difficult for him to find the time to write down a whole book of what he wants to share with the young and old readers. When I came up with the idea of producing this book from recorded interviews, he welcomed it. So my first step was to make a long list of questions on the subject matter and hold a number of Q&A sessions with him to obtain his answers. After these were organised into various chapters, he gladly filled in the gaps with his written responses that considerably added to the value of the volume. With his good humour, he is always appreciative of any new ideas to improve and enhance the core message of this book.

Since attention spans have been getting shorter and shorter with 24-hour TV channels and overtly illustrated popular media, special effort has been made to include a good number of graphics. Not only do they catch the eye but also provide an overview of the content when one merely flips through the pages of this book. Hopefully, it will result in reading all of it.

Creating this book from recorded interviews, adding and editing to the text, looking up recent events and developments and devising illustrations has been a challenging but satisfying task. It seemed some special energy powered and accelerated this project to complete it in a matter of a few weeks after the entire edited text was accidentally deleted in the innards of my personal computer!

It may seem that the combination of a spiritual leader who was a top corporate executive in his previous career and a former Business Editor who has delved into spirituality for many decades is unique in creating this book. But it is not so. In fact, in the early 20th century, an outstanding Russian spiritual leader, George Gurjjeff, attracted a leading journalist and author, P. D. Ouspensky, who wrote five books on the life and thoughts of the spiritual leader. In line with this tradition, it is hoped that this book will also reach out to as many readers over as much time.

Kul Bhushan

kb@kulbhushan.net

2015.

Mahabharata

The Greatest of All The Epics

The greatest of all the epics, The Mahabharata, is seven times longer than *The Iliad* and *The Odyssey* combined. Its author is the great sage Krishna Dwaipayana Vyasa aka Veda Vyasa (literally the compiler). It is said to contain every type of human relationship on this earth. With 100,000 couplets, it relates the story of enmity between two groups of cousins that culminated in a terrible war.

The cousins are the children of two brothers of the Bharata clan. Bharat, the ancient name of India, comes from the Emperor Bharata, son of Rishabhadeva. When he ruled, the whole planet earth was known as Bharatavarsha. Two brothers, Dhritarashtra and Pandu, were born in the Kuru Dynasty. The conflict starts when the elder one, Dhritarashtra, could not become the king as he was born blind. So the younger one, Pandu, was crowned king.

Dhritarashtra fathered a hundred sons, the eldest being Duryodhana, while Pandu had five sons namely, Yudhishthira, Bhima, Arjuna, Nakula and Sahadeva, known as Pandavas.

Since King Pandu died at an early age, Dhritarashtra became a caretaker king. Pandu's widow Kunti and her five children were provided shelter by Dhritarashtra. So both the Kauravas (the sons of Dhritarashtra) and the five Pandava sons grew up together in the same royal environment.

As Kshatriyas, all of them were well trained in martial arts by Guru Drona, an expert in archery. Bhishma, the senior most member of the Kuru clan, oversaw all aspects of the upbringing of both the Kaurava and the Pandava children.

The Kauravas, especially Duryodhana, was very jealous of the Pandava brothers for he knew that ultimately the Pandavas will acquire the right to rule the kingdom. Therefore, right from his boyhood, he tried many ploys to kill all of them. Undaunted in his efforts to eliminate them despite repeated failures, he knew he had the backing of his father, Dhritarashtra, who also secretly desired his son Duryodhana to become the king and not Yudhishthira, the eldest Pandava.

The Supreme Lord Krishna, descended on this planet at this time, appearing as a prince in the Yadu dynasty. His father, Vasudeva, is the brother of Kunti, the widow of King Pandu and the mother of the Pandavas. The Lord always protected the pious Pandavas from different dangerous situations. When all attempts failed to kill them, Duryodhana dealt a master stroke by inviting the Pandavas for a gambling session. As Kshatriyas, they were obliged to accept the invitation, and so participated in this gambling. The wicked Duryodhana, with the help of his cunning maternal uncle Shakuni, cheated the Pandavas in the dice game. Yudhishthira lost everything, including his kingdom. When he had nothing left to play with, he staked his chaste wife Draupadi and lost. Duryodhana then summoned Draupadi to the open court and tried to strip her. Despite her desperate pleadings, no one - her five husbands nor the respected elders - could stop Duryodhana. Totally helpless, she then prayed to the Supreme Lord Krishna who came to her rescue. After this humiliation, the Pandavas were forced to go into exile for thirteen years, according to an earlier gambling stake.

On completing the exile, the Pandavas rightfully claimed their share of kingdom but Duryodhana refused flatly. To avert a disastrous war, Lord Krishna went Himself as Pandavas' messenger to the court of Dhritarashtra to plead for a peaceful settlement. Duryodhana would have none of it. Overcome by anger, greed and envy, and disregarding the universally accepted diplomatic immunity to envoys, Duryodhana plotted to kill the Lord Himself.

But the Lord, being the super soul situated in the hearts of all living beings, exposed Duryodhana's trickery. The Lord impressed upon Dhritarashtra that since the Kshatriyas were obliged not to engage in any other occupation except political and administrative duties, the Pandavas should be given to rule at least five villages. Duryodhana interrupted this proposal to ridicule Lord Krishna's attempt at negotiation and sneered that the Pandavas would not be given a piece of land as big as a pin-cushion. Then, the Lord partially displayed His Universal Form to the court to show the ominous direction in which the Kauravas were hurtling. Thus, a war among the cousins became inevitable.

As Lord Krishna was related to both the Kauravas and the Pandavas through matrimonial alliances, He declared that He would not fight on behalf of either side. However, he offered the choice between his Yadava army or His personal services as a guide and counsellor to both the parties. The wicked Duryodhana opted for the Lord's army, the pious Pandavas were gratified to have the Lord's moral support. Thus Krishna became the charioteer for Arjuna, the Pandavas' commander in chief in the great Mahabharata War on the battlefield of Kurukshetra.

Before this war could begin, Arjuna had second thoughts. The greatest warrior of his age, Arjuna, requested Lord Krishna to position his chariot between the two armies ready to fight. He laid down his famous bow and arrows and, as he surveyed the field full of his kinsmen, his cousins and his gurus, he was filled with sadness to start killing them. He confessed to Lord Krishna that he did not want to fight his own loved ones.

At this crossroads, Lord Krishna persuaded Arjuna to stand up and perform his '*dharma*' or duty like a true warrior or Khastriya. The ebb and flow of the dialogue between the two, forms the 18 chapters of the Bhagavat Gita or the Divine Song. In the course of this repartee, Lord Krishna reveals His true and unlimited universalform and ultimately at the end of the discourse, he surrenders unconditionally to The Lord. In the Gita forms the core of ancient Indian wisdom that was relevant 5,000 years ago and is equally relevant now. This scripture is the magnificent legacy of this apparently great tragedy. In Gita, the Lord provides clear guidelines to all living beings of this world on how they should lead their lives on this earth and ultimately attain release.

With the Supreme Lord Krishna guiding, Arjuna and the Pandavas win the 18-day war as the victory for truth and what is right.

Mahabharata's Main Characters

The Supreme Lord

Krishna, son of King Vasudeva by Devaki, and brother of Subhadra, the second wife of Arjuna

The Ancestors

- *Shantanu*, great-grandfather of Kauravas and Pandavas
- *Bhishma Pitamah*, grand-uncle of Kauravas and Pandavas
- *Kripacharya*, guru of Kauravas and Pandavas
- *Parashurama*, guru of Bhishma
- *Dronacharya*, guru of Kauravas and Pandavas, teacher of martial arts.
- *Ashwasthama*, son of Dronacharya
- *Vyasa*, son of sage Parashara and composer of Mahabharata

The Pandavas	*The Kauravas*
Pandu, father of Pandavas	*Dhritarashtra*, blind father of 100 Kauravas
Kunti, Pandu's first wife	*Gandhari*, wife of Dhritarashtra and mother of Kauravas
Madri, Pandu's second wife	*Duryodhana*, eldest son of Dhritarashtra
The Five Pandava Brothers	*Dushashana*, second son of Dhritarashtra
1. *Yudhistra*, the eldest Pandava, son of demi-god Dharma	*Vidura*, advisor to Dhritarashtra
	Shakuni brother of Gandhari and maternal uncle of Dhritarashtra
2. *Bhima*, son of demi-god Vayu	*Karna*, son of Kunti but adopted by a charioteer
3. *Arjuna*, son of demi-god Indra	*Pariksit Grandson of Arjun*

4. *Nakula*, on of demi-god Ashwini Kumaras

5. *Sahadeva*, son of demi-god Ashwini Kumaras

Draupadi, the wife of five Pandavas

Abhimanyu, son of Arjuna

Shikandi, daughter of King Draupada, later became a man, ally of Pandavas

Ghatotkacha, Bhima's son

Dhrishtadyumna, brother of Draupadi

Satyaki, charioteer of Krishna

Bhurishrava, son of King Somadatta

Parikshit, grandson of Arjuna

Kurukshetra War: The Commanders

The Kauravas	***The Pandavas***
1. *Bhishma*	1. *Arjun*
2. *Dronyacharya*	2. *Bhima*
3. *Karana*	3. *Dhrishtadymna*
4. *Shalya*	4. *Abhimanyu*
5. *Kripacharya*	5. *Ghatotkacha*
6. *Ashwasthama*	6. *Shikhandi*
7. *Duryodhana*	7. *Satyaki*

Command and Control

Kauravas: Kauravas: Centralized leadership. One Head of Army at a time, who has supreme authority of 11.

Pandavas: Distributed leadership. Seven commanders for the seven divisions or *akshouhini*.

Krishna – Chief Counselor and Arjuna's charioteer.

Arjuna –Supreme Commander in Chief.

1. Virata (King of Matsya).
2. Drupada (King of Pancala).
3. Sahadeva(King of Magadha).
4. Dhrishtaketu (King of Chedi).
5. Satyaki (Only warrior from Dwarka).

6. Shikhandi (Prince of Pancala).

7. Dhrishtadymna – Commander in Chief.

Strategy

Kauravas: No team spirit, all fought their individual wars.

Bhishma: For his Vow to protect the throne Hastinapur.

Drona and Kripa: Owed allegiance to the throne.

Shalya: Originally a Pandava ally, cheated by Duryodhana to be in the Kauravas Camp..

Karna: To prove his mantle against Arjuna and for his friendship for Duryodhana.

Bhishma and Karna. Bhishma and Shakuni. Karna and Shakuni. Karna and Shalya. Shalya and Bhishma did not fight as a team.

Pandavas: Fought as one team with one Goal, victory. All had great respect for Lord Krishna and Yudhishthira. As warriors, they were in complete awe of Bhima and Arjuna. Most of them were close relatives and all were part of the decision-making process.

Implementation

Kauravas: Except for Duryodhana, nobody wanted the war.

The four main generals had strong ties with the Pandavas.

Bhishma: Won't kill the Panadavas but kill a thousand soldiers each day.

Drona: Won't kill the Pandavas but only capture them only.

Shalya (Nakula-Shadeva's maternal uncle): Loved the Pandavas and covertly helped them by humiliating Karna.

Karna (brother to the Pandavas): Promised not to kill any of the Pandavas except Arjuna.

Pandavas: Common goal. But the individuals had their individual targets. Their own agenda, which just became one with the teams' agenda.

Dhratsadyumna: Drona.

Shikhandi: Bhishma.

Satayaki – Bhurisravas.

Arjuna – Karna.

Bhima – Duryodhana and his brothers.

Sahadeva – Shakuni and his sons.

Nakula – Karna's sons.

The Right team is made by selecting the Right Individuals. Get the right man for the right job.

War Strategy

Kurukshetra War: *The Commanders*

The Kauravas

1. *Bhishma*
2. *Dronyacharya*
3. *Karana*
4. *Shalya*
5. *Kripacharya*
6. *Ashwasthama*
7. *Duryodhana*

The Pandavas

1. *Arjuna*
2. *Bhima*
3. *Dhrishtadymna*
4. *Abhimanyu*
5. *Ghatotkacha*
6. *Shikhandi*
7. *Satyaki*

Command and Control

Kauravas: Centralized leadership. One Head of Army at a time, who has supreme authority of 11 akshouhini of army. Bhishma, Drona, Karna, Shalya and Ashwatthama.

Pandavas: Distributed leadership. Seven commanders for the seven divisions or *akshouhini*.

Krishna – Chief Counsellor and Arjuna's charioteer.

Arjuna –Supreme Commander in Chief.

1. Virat (King of Matsya).

2. Drupad (King of Pancala).

3. Sahadeva(King of Magadha).

4. Dhrshtaketu (King of Chedi).

5. Satyaki (Only warrior from Dwarka).

6. Shikhandi (Prince of Pancala).

7. Dhrshtadymna – Commander in Chief.

Strategy

Kauravas: No team spirit, all fought their individual wars.

Bhishma: For his Vow to protect the throne Hastinapur.

Drona and Kripa: Owed allegiance to the throne.

Shalya: Originally a Pandava ally, cheated by Duryodhana to be in the Kauravas Camp.

Karna: To prove his mantle against Arjuna and for his friendship for Duryodhana.

Bhishma and Karna. Bhishma and Shakuni. Karna and Shakuni. Karna and Shalya. Shalya and Bhishma did not fight as a team.

Pandavas: Fought as one team with one Goal, victory. All had great respect for Lord Krishna and Yudhishthira. As warriors, they were in complete awe of Bhima and Arjuna. Most of them were close relatives and all were part of the decision-making process.

Implementation

Kauravas: Except for Duryodhana, nobody wanted the war.

The four main generals had strong ties with the Pandavas.

Bhishma: Won't kill the Panadavas but kill a thousand soldiers each day.

Drona: Won't kill the Pandavas but only capture them only.

Shalya (Nakula-Shadeva's maternal uncle): Loved the Pandavas and covertly helped them by humiliating Karna.

Karna (brother to the Pandavas): Promised not to kill any of the Pandavas except Arjuna.

Pandavas:

Lord Krishna the greatest crisis manager ever.

Common goal. But the individuals had their own agenda which became common with the team agenda.

Dhratsadyumna : Drona.

Shikhandi : Bhishma.

Satayaki – Bhurisravas.

Arjuna – Karna.

Bhima – Duryodhana and his brothers.

Sahadeva – Shakuni and his sons.

Nakula –Karna's sons.

Woman Power

Kauravas: Patriarchal structure. Bhishma, Drona, Kripa, Dhratarashtra, Vidur, Shakuni, Duryodhana, Karna, Duhsasana. No women in the decision making process. Gandhari retreated to the Inner Chambers. Nobody listened to her.

Pandavas: Matriarchal Structure.

Kunti was the authority for the Pandavas.

"Whatever my mother says is Dharma to me," said Yudhishthira.

Draupadi was a companion in whatever the Pandavas did. She had a big role in all the decision making.

Even the younger Pandavas : Ghatotkacha, Abhimanyu and Iravan were brought up by their mothers.

The Bhagavat Gita

Your Masterplan from God Himself

If you want a master plan for your life, if you want advice when you are in a dilemma, if you want inspiration when you are depressed, if you want a constant companion that keeps on revealing new and deeper meanings for your life, or if your mind is always full of questions with no answers, then this one book, the *Bhagavat Gita*, is enough. Why? Because God Himself, appearing the self-same taking the divine form of Lord Krishna, explains the mysteries and guides you today as He did 5,000 years ago.

The *Gita's* message is timeless and beyond all religions. Its dialogue between Lord Krishna and His friend and devotee Arjuna, is also taking place within the heart and soul of every human being on the battlefield of this terrible and beautiful world. The *Gita* should not be read as a book by some mundane author but approached slowly and repeatedly bringing your inner and outer experiences to understand its deeper meanings, and finding solutions to the disturbing questions of your life as well as for the ultimate goal of spiritual emancipation.

Ch 01 - Observing Armies Poised to Fight

The greatest warrior of the Pandavas, Arjuna, sees his gurus, cousins and friends lined up against him on the battlefield in Kuruskshetra, to kill or be killed. Overcome by grief and pity, he is in a dilemma. How can he fight and kill them? And what will be the value of his victory if none of them would be alive to share his joy? He lays down his Gandiva, his mighty bow, and arrows, unwilling to fight, seeking guidance from Lord Krishna.

Ch 02 - Physical Body and Eternal Soul

Lord Krishna responds by asking why he is disheartened and hopeless during this crisis when, as a warrior, his duty is to fight. The Lord explains the basic difference between the temporary physical body and the eternal spiritual soul. Lord Krishna outlines the importance of duty (dharma) and the honour of a warrior, the process of transmigration, the nature of selfless service to the Supreme and the qualities of an enlightened person.

Ch 03 - Karma Yoga - Action and Reaction

Arjuna asks, if selfless service to the Supreme and becoming enlightened is the goal of life, why then is Lord Krishna asking him to do a cruel deed. Lord Krishna responds that everyone must engage in some activity in the world but actions can bind one or liberate one from this world. By acting in service to and for the pleasure of the Supreme, one can be freed from the law of *karma* (action and reaction) and attain transcendental knowledge of the self and the Supreme.

Ch 04 - Spiritual Knowledge of Soul and God

Lord Krishna imparts transcendental knowledge—spiritual knowledge of the soul, God, and their relationship and how it purifies and liberates. This knowledge is the fruit of karma yoga or selfless devotional action, says Lord Krishna, and explains the purpose of His periodic descents to the material world, and the necessity of surrendering to an enlightened guru or master.

Ch 05 - Karma Yoga: Path to Bliss

Arjuna wants a clear answer on what course to follow: renounce all actions or perform them. Lord Krishna explains that the path is to perform all actions in the physical world outwardly but renouncing their fruits for personal enjoyment but offered to the Lord . Then the wise person becomes purified by transcendental knowledge, attains peace, detachment, forbearance, spiritual vision and bliss.

Ch 06 - Dhyan Yoga

Lord Krishna further explains the meditative practice (dhyan yoga) to control the senses and the mind and focus one's concentration on the Supersoul, the form of Lord Krishna situated in everyone's heart. This practice culminates in '*samadhi*'—the full consciousness of the Supreme. But Arjuna says it is difficult to control the fickle mind. Lord Krishna advises him to go beyond passion and make practice with a sense of detachment for this purpose.

Ch 07 - Knowing the Absolute

Lord Krishna describes the essential attributes of God as the supreme Truth, the supreme cause and the sustaining force of everything, both material and spiritual. After describing the different types of devotees, the Lord says that advanced souls surrender to Him in devotion, while impious souls divert their minds to other objects of worship.

Ch 08 - Attaining the Supreme

Arjuna wants to know what is Brahman or the Supreme. Lord Krishna says that He is the Supreme Brahman and that by remembering Him in devotion throughout one's life and especially at the time of one's death, one can attain His supreme abode, beyond the material world.

Ch 09 - Most Secret Knowledge

Now that Arjuna is ready, Lord Krishna reveals to him the most secret knowledge that He Himself is the God and the ultimate source of everything. Hence, He is the supreme object of worship. The soul is eternally related to Him through devotion. So those who are solely devoted to Him attain their rewards in liberation.

Ch 10 - Opulence of the Absolute

Arjuna asks Lord Krishna how he can know Him with His divine energies. Lord Krishna outlines his energies of beauty, grandeur, sublimity in the material and the spiritual worlds. As the supreme cause of all causes and the support and essence of everything, Lord Krishna is the supreme object of worship for all beings.

Ch 11 - The Universal Form

After Arjuna requests Lord Krishna to reveal his divine opulences, the Lord reveals His spectacular, unlimited form as the entire cosmic universe and time to establish his divinity beyond all doubt.

He explains that his beautiful human-like form is the original form of Godhead. One can perceive this form only through pure devotion. Arjuna is overwhelmed and requests the Lord again to assume His humanlike form, which He does.

Ch 12 - Bhakti Yoga: Devotional Service

Arjuna wants to know who are more perfect: those who follow loving devotion (Bhagti) or those who worship the unmanifest (His impersonal Brahman feature)? Lord Krishna answers that the highest and the fastest means to attain pure love and the highest state of spiritual existence is Bhakti Yoga. Those who follow this supreme path develop divine qualities. He enumerates the qualities of the person whom He loves the most. The Lord establishes that the worship by Bhakti Yoga is the most perfect.

Ch 13 - Nature, The Enjoyer and Consciousness

Arjuna wants to know what nature is. Who is the person? What is the 'field' or the body? And who is the enjoyer of the field? Lord Krishna explains these concepts of matter and spirit and His universal presence in all. One who understands the difference between the physical body, the soul and the Supersoul beyond them attains liberation from this material world.

Ch 14 - Three Modes of Material Nature

All embodied souls are influenced, governed and controlled by three modes or qualities of material nature. These are goodness, passion and ignorance. Lord Krishna explains these three modes, how they influence us, and how one can go beyond them and the qualities of one who has attained the transcendental state.

Ch 15 - Yoga of the Supreme Person

Lord Krishna describes this material world as a Banyan tree with roots above and the branches below as its reflection in water. The ultimate purpose of Vedic knowledge is to detach oneself from this material world and to understand that Lord Krishna is the Supreme Personality of Godhead. One who understands Lord Krishna as the Supreme Personality of Godhead and surrenders to Him, engages in loving service to Him, attains the transcendental stage.

Ch 16 - Divine and Demonic Natures

Lord Krishna outlines the cardinal virtues and the deadly sins. Those who do not follow the scriptures and whimsically live demonic lives, are reborn at a lower level and in further material bondage. But those who possess divine virtues and live regulated lives, abiding by the authority of the scriptures, generally attain spiritual liberation finally after abandoning the three gates of hell: lust, anger and greed.

Ch 17 - Divisions of Faith

Arjuna asks, 'What about those persons who forsake the authority of the scriptures and offer sacrifice filled with faith?' Lord Krishna answers that there are three types of faith, corresponding to and evolving from the three modes of material nature. The actions of those guided by passion and ignorance result only in impermanent material results. The actions of those guided by goodness according to the authority of the scriptures, purify the heart and lead to pure faith in Lord Krishna and devotion to Him.

Ch 18 - Perfection of Renunciation and Surrender

Arjuna wants to know the truth about renunciation and surrender to the Lord. The true meaning of renunciation, the three modes of nature and their effects on all human activities are explained by Lord Krishna. He also indicates the method to achieve the realization of the Supreme or Brahman, and the qualifications of the recipients of the glories of the *Bhagavat Gita*. Lord Krishna concludes by saying that the highest path of religion is absolute, unconditional and loving surrender to Lord Krishna. This will free one from all sins, bring complete enlightenment and enable one to return to the abode of the Lord. After dispelling his doubts and confusions, Arjuna says he has regained the proper way of thinking and is ready to do the Lord's bidding.

The *Gita's* core teaching is that we should surrender only to Lord Krishna unconditionally.

Progressive Stages

The three different paths explained in the *Gita* are nothing but progressive stages that necessarily culminate in Bhakti. These different paths like karma, jnana, dhyana form a part of bhakti and their goals do not exist separately. Nishkama karma yoga (action without desiring to enjoy the results but offered to the Lord) is for those whose minds are impure with innumerable worldly desires. Jnana yoga (the path of knowledge and contemplation) is suitable for those whose minds are free from enjoying material comforts or luxuries. Those who have theoretical spiritual knowledge after becoming free from material contamination, are qualified for the contemplative life of dhyana yoga (spiritual meditation on the divinity within). When pursued further, all paths lead one to the final stage of bhakti yoga, the transcendental loving devotional service to the Supreme Lord Krishna.

When we follow the path of action, it is called Karma Yoga, when we proceed through introspection, it is known as Jnana Yoga, when go into meditation, it is termed as Dhyana yoga, and rendering loving service is described as Bhakti yoga. Bhakti yoga is the real means for complete liberation. In the initial stage of endeavour, one may take to any of these paths according to one's inherited nature, but ultimately one reaches the Bhakti yoga. The Lord emphatically says in the *Gita* (18/55), 'Only through devotional service can one understand Me as I am.' This is the essential teaching of the *Gita*.

Who is Qualified to Comment on the Gita?

Today, innumerable translations and commentaries are available in many languages on Gita worldwide including many scholastic interpretations with purely an academic approach. It is a most unfortunate fact is that most of them do not acknowledge Lord Krishna as the Supreme God. Many commentators condescendingly accord him the status of a Superman with a super brain, explaining complex philosophy but never acknowledging his Godhood.

Not to be left behind, many eminent Vedic scholars and renowned Indian intellectuals do not deem it necessary to recognise Lord Krishna as God. This is because most of these commentators belong to 'yogic' and 'jnani' schools of thought based on the erroneous and mistaken philosophy of the ultimate reality as an impersonal abstract absolute, without any transcendental personality and attributes.

Any commentary or translation of the Gita should highlight, reiterate and reinforce the main objective of the scripture throughout the work. Lord Krishna imparts the divine message of the Gita Surrender to Him with loving devotional service to Him is the subject matter of Gita, and the love of Krishna is the goal of Gita. Every reader of Gita can easily understand this overall objective of Lord Krishna's discourse in the Gita.

However, the so-called scholars, with sectarian bias and their misunderstandings, invariably provide trivial distortions that obscure the original objective and deliberately dilute the overall intention and meaning of this scripture. These half baked attempts at spirituality are often undertaken by so called pseudo Vedic scholars and Sanskrit pundits only to show off their academic brilliance and scholastic ability. Tragically, they end to eclipse the true glory of the original text. The great work of the Gita is a sad victim to this. All these commentators desire fame and recognition with the help of Gita without acknowledging Lord Krishna as God. It is like desiring to enjoy the kingdom of God without God.

But, this is nothing strange to the world of devotees because the Lord has amply clarified in the Gita (4/3) as to who is the real candidate to perfect understanding as follows:

Sa evayam may ate dya Yogah proktah puratanah
bhakto si me sakha ceti rahasyam hy etad uttamam

That very ancient science of the relationship with the Supreme is today told by Me to you because you are My devotee as well as My friend and can therefore understand the transcendental mystery of this science. A genuine spiritual seeker will therefore do well to strictly follow and understand the true intention and significance of the Gita written by fully surrendered devotees of the Lord who have realized the truth to derive immense spiritual benefit. The Lord himself insists this in the Gita (4/34):

tad viddhi pranipatena pariprasnena sevaya
upadeksyanti te jnanam jnaninas tattva-darsinah

Just try to learn the truth by approaching a spiritual master, inquire from him submissively and render service unto him. The self-realised souls can impart knowledge unto you because they have seen the truth.

The Lord, therefore, periodically deputes his spiritual ambassadors to this planet to propagate the science and the spirituality of Gita. Therefore, only great Acharyas, the spiritual teachers in the Vaishnava tradition, including the liberated souls of Gaudiya Vaishnava lineage, have properly projected the unadulterated meaning of Lord Krishna's dialogue with Arjuna in the Gita. Why? Because only they have actual spiritual contact with the Lord.

Does the Gita Promote Violence?

It is believed that over eight million warriors were killed in the 18-day battle of Kurukshetra. Before this humongous battle began, the commander Arjuna laid down his bow and arrows and wanted to go away. His friend and charioteer Lord Krishna convinced him to stand up to evil and fight. So, did the Lord Krishna, with his message of the *Gita*, cause all this violence?

This, unfortunately, is a very wrong notion, very widespread since a very long time about the core teaching of the *Gita*. No, this is a thorough misunderstanding. A great warrior like Arjuna, endowed with the true nature of Kshatriya spirit, was not likely to show compassion for the wrong reasons, that too, in the critical situation on the battlefield. He did not envisage this earlier.

On the contrary, he had been looking forward to that day enthusiastically. During his thirteen years of exile with his brothers, he was collecting arms and weapons, eagerly waiting to completely smash all his opponents to rightfully claim their legitimate kingdom usurped cunningly by Duryodhana and his brothers. The reality is that Arjuna's physical concept of life, that existed deep within him, suddenly surfaced when he surveyed the warriors lined up opposite him. After all, they were his revered gurus and his cousins. So he moaned in the *Gita* (1/32 to 35):

Kim no rajyenagovinda Kim bhogairjivitenava
Yesamarthekanksitam no rajyambhogahsukhanica
Taimevasthitayuddhepranamstyaktvadhananica
Acaryahpitarahputrastathaivacapitamahah

Matulahsvasurahpautrahsyalahsambandhinastatha
Etannahantumicchamighnato pi madhusudana
Apitrailokya-rajyasyahetohkim nu mahi-krte
Nihatyadhartarastran nah kapritihsyajjanrdana

'O Govinda, of what avail to us are a kingdom, happiness or even life itself when all those for whom we may desire them are now arrayed on this battlefield? O Madhusudana, when teachers, fathers, sons, grandfathers, maternal uncles, fathers-in-law, grandsons, brothers-in-law and other relatives are ready to give up their lives and properties and are standing before me, why should I wish to kill them, even though they might otherwise kill me? O maintainer of all living entities, I am not prepared to fight with them even in exchange for the three worlds, let alone this wrath. What pleasure will we derive from killing the sons of Dhrtarashtra?'

It is just like a common man who enjoys by throwing a champagne party for his closest friends and relatives when he achieves an extraordinary success or receives a huge windfall. On such occasions, hobnobbing in their company, he revels and rejoices in receiving accolades and adulations.

Positioned between the two armies, it suddenly occurred to Arjuna that all the warriors standing on both sides were brave Kshatriyas, and none of them would flee the battlefield. They would either kill or get killed. In such a situation, all of them would be totally wiped out, leaving nobody alive to share the joy of the Pandavas' victory. Therefore, he confided to Krishna: What is the use of gaining this victory? Precisely for this reason, the Lord began His discourse to dispel Arjuna's misconception that he is only the body. The Lord detected that His friend's physical idea and the resulting sense of gratification are the true causes of his misplaced compassion, unworthy of a Kshatriya. This idea became the impediment even in executing his duty based on the bodily conception of life. The Lord was very articulate when he addressed Arjuna in the*Gita* (18/60) thus:

Svabhava-jenakaunteyaNibaddhahsvenakarmana
KartumnecchasiyanmohatKarisyasyavaso pi tat

'Under illusion, you are declining to fight, but compelled by the work born of your nature (Kshatriya), you will have to be engaged in warfare, O Son of Kunti.'

Thus it is clear the Lord was not promoting violence because he was clearly aware that Arjuna's disinclination to fight was temporary due to illusory misidentification of the physical body as the self. The Lord was merely advising him to perform his duty, failing which he would commit a sin due to non-performance of scripturally prescribed duty for *kshatriyas* according to *varnaashrama*, the social principles strictly followed by the society then.

Thus, the Supreme Lord was only encouraging Arjuna to fight the war as a matter of duty without any other consideration since Arjuna was not a spiritually liberated person. Hence, the Supreme Lord's advice should not be misconstrued for words that promote violence.

Comments on the Gita and the Supreme Lord Krishna

Albert Einstein, *Nuclear Physicist and Nobel Laureate, (1879 -1955):*

'When I read the *Bhagavad Gita* and reflect about how God created this universe everything else seems so superfluous.'

'We owe a lot to the Indians, who taught us how to count, without which no worthwhile scientific discovery could have been made.'

J. Robert Oppenheimer, *American Nuclear Physicist (1904-1967):*

On witnessing the incredible violence and the power of the first atomic bomb test, he recalled lines from the *Bhagavad Gita*: 'Now I am become Death, the destroyer of worlds.' A Sanskrit scholar and an avid reader of this scripture, he always kept the *Gita* on his table and gifted it to many people.

Ralph Waldo Emerson, *American Philosopher (1803-1882):*

'I owed a magnificent day to the *Bhagavad Gita*. It was the first of books; it was as if an empire spoke to us, nothing small or unworthy, but large, serene, consistent, the voice of an old intelligence which in another age and climate had pondered and thus disposed of the same questions which exercise us.'

Arthur Schopenhauer, *German Philosopher (1788-1860):*

'In the whole world there is no study so beneficial and so elevating as that of the Upanishads. It has been the solace of my life—it will be the solace of my death.'

'It is the most rewarding and the most elevating book which can be possible in the world.

Henry David Thoreau, *American Philosopher (1817-1862):*

'...In the morning I bathe my intellect in the stupendous and cosmological philosophy of the *Bhagavad-Gita* in comparison with which our modern world and its literature seem puny and trivial.'

'...Whenever I have read any part of the Vedas, I have felt that some unearthly and unknown light illuminated me. In the great teaching of the Vedas, there is no touch of the sectarianism. It is of ages, climes, and nationalities and is the royal road for the attainment of the Great Knowledge. When I am at it, I feel that I am under the spangled heavens of a summer night.'

Aldous Huxley, *English Author (1894-1963):*

'*Bhagavad Gita* is the most systematic statement of spiritual evolution of endowing value to mankind. It is one of the most clear and comprehensive summaries of perennial philosophy ever revealed; hence its enduring value is subject not only to India but to all of humanity.'

Mahatma Gandhi, *Father of the Indian Nation (1869-1948):*

'When doubts haunt me, when disappointments stare me in the face, and I see not one ray of hope on the horizon, I turn to *Bhagavad Gita* and find a verse to comfort me; and I immediately begin to smile in the midst of overwhelming sorrow. Those who meditate on the *Gita* will derive fresh joy and new meanings from it every day.'

Jawaharlal Nehru, *India's First Prime Minister (1889 -1964):*

'The *Bhagavad Gita* deals essentially with the spiritual foundation of human existence. It is a call of action to meet the obligations and duties of life; yet keeping in view the spiritual nature and grander purpose of the universe.'

Hermann Hesse, *German Author (1877-1962):*

'The marvel of the *Bhagavad Gita* is its truly beautiful revelation of life's wisdom which enables philosophy to blossom into religion.'

Dr Albert Schweitzer, *German Author, Musician, Medical Doctor, Nobel Laureate (1875-1965):*

'The *Bhagavad Gita* has a profound influence on the spirit of mankind by its devotion to God which is manifested by actions.'

Sri Aurobindo, *Poet, Philosopher, Writer, Indian Spiritual Master (1872 - 1950):*

'*Bhagavad Gita* is a true scripture of the human race a living creation rather than a book, with a new message for every age and a new meaning for every civilization.'

Carl Jung, *Swiss Psychiatrist (1875-1961):*

'The idea that man is like unto an inverted tree seems to have been current in bygone ages. The link with Vedic conceptions is provided by Plato in his *Timaeus* in which it states, 'Behold we are not an earthly but a heavenly plant.' This correlation can be discerned by what Krishna expresses in chapter 15 of *Bhagavad Gita*.'

German Philosophers *in the late 18th and early 19th Centuries:*

The *Bhagavad Gita* influenced many notable German philosophers in Germany including Friedrich and August Schlegel, Wilhelm von Humboldt, Arthur Schopenhauer, Friedrich Nietzsche and GWF Hegel. Schopenhauer kept the *Gita*, rather than the *Bible*, on his bedside table and would read from it most nights. His interest in the *Gita* clearly influenced many who came after him, especially Friedrich Nietzsche.

Shrimad Bhagavatam:

The First Encyclopaedia

Shrimad Bhagavatam, also known as *Bhagavat Purana* or simply as *Bhagavat*, covers all subjects of interest to mankind and the description of the entire life of Lord Krishna. This scripture written as poetry, arranged in twelve sections or cantos, has 335 chapters with about 18,000 verses. A 'purana' contains historical accounts and *Bhagavat Purana* is accepted as the most important, detailed and complete in Hindu scripture.

Its primary focus is 'bhakti' or personal devotion to the Supreme Lord Krishna who is the fountainhead of variousin carnations,including Lord Vishnu. The epic poem describes the transcendental pastimes of the birth, childhood, and the youthof the Supreme Lord until His disappearance. All forms of bhakti, its practice and analysis are also included. The scripture gives the knowledge of the absolute truth, the transcendental science delineating various aspects of the ultimate reality and details of spiritual abodes. Like an encyclopaedia, it contains arts and architecture, atomic science, astrology, astronomy, chemistry, cosmology, culture, economics, education, embryology, evolution theory, mathematics, physics, political administration, religion, warfare and many more sciences.

This Mahapurana (great history) was written 5,000 years ago by the great sage Veda Vyasa, described as 'the literary incarnation of God'. After writing the four Vedas and the Upanishads , Veda Vyasa put these in a summaryform, known as Vedanta or Brahma Sutra. Anticipatingthat it could be misinterpreted in the future, Veda Vyasa wrote Bhagavatam as a natural commentary. Thus, it has been described as 'the ripened fruit of the tree of the Vedas'. This great epic was first spoken by Veda Vyasa to his enlightened son Shukadevaat Badarika Ashramam. Later, the great Emperor Parikshit heard it from Shukadeva for seven days at Shuktal, near Delhi. Shri Suta, a disciple of Shukadeva, explained this scripture to an assembly of 60,000 sages at Naimisharanya, near Lucknow.

It is said that Veda Vyasa was advised to go into a trance (*samadhi*) by practising Bhakti Yoga and see for himself the entire life of Lord Krishna. So the great sage started to meditate in his cottage in Shamyaprasa on the banks of the river Saraswati. Due to his intensity in Bhakti Yoga, the Supreme Lord Krishna appeared with His divine consort Radha, representing the spiritual energy. The goddess Durga, the embodiment of material energy, also appeared in the background. In his trance, he also observed innumerable living entities that constitute the marginal energy of the Supreme Lord suffering and struggling due to bewildering influences of material energy. Afflicted by this, they were forced to forget their real identity as spirit souls. Thus, they were made to believe that they were merely physical bodies.

Since every living entity is basically spiritual the material miseries are superfluous; so these can be mitigated by direct devotional service (Bhakti Yoga) to Lord Krishna. As most people do not know this, the learned Veda Vyasa, coming out of samadhi, wrote this magnificent devotional piece of work,*Bhagavata Mahapurana*, after complete realization of the Absolute Transcendental Truth—Lord Krishna.

This can be easily understood by the fact that although this literature contains twelve cantos with many chapters, the tenth canto has the maximum of 90 chapters with a full and a detailed description of the transcendental pastimes of Lord Krishna. The most important fact, however, is that Shri Suta, during his discourse to the assembly of 60,000 sages while enumerating twenty-two of God's main incarnations, establishes the '*Svayam Bhagavan*' status of Lord Krishna as the original Personality of Godhead. This means that the Lord is the source of all incarnations.

WHY LORD KRISHNA IS SUPREME?

Because He alone has the total of 64 attributes of the Manifestation of The Supreme and He excels in everything

1. Beautiful Physical Features
2. Auspicious Characteristics
3. Pleasing
4. Effulgent
5. Strong
6. Ever Youthful
7. Wonderful Linguist
8. Truthful
9. Pleasing Talker
10. Fluent
11. Highly Learned
12. Highly Intelligent
13. Genius
14. Artistic
15. Clever
16. Expert
17. Grateful
18. Determined
19. Expert Judge of Time and Circumstance
20. Seer by the Authority of the Scriptures
21. Pure
22. Self Controlled
23. Steadfast
24. Forbearing
25. Forgiving
26. Grave
27. Self-satisfied
28. Possessing Equilibrium
29. Magnanimous
30. Religious
31. Heroic
32. Compassionate
33. Respectful
34. Gentle
35. Liberal
36. Shy
37. Protector of Surrendered Souls
38. Happy

KRISHNA

VISHNU

SHIVA

BRAHMA

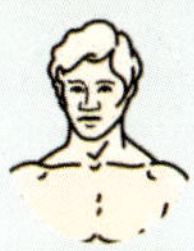

HUMANS

39. Well-wisher of His Devotees
40. Controlled by Love
41. All-auspicious
42. Most Powerful
43. Famous
44. Popular
45. Specially attractive for Devotees
46. Very Attractive for Women
47. All-worshippable
48. All Opulent
49. All Honourable
50. The Supreme Controller
51. Changeless
52. All Cognizant
53. Ever Fresh
54. Eternal Conscious Blissful Form
55. Possessing All Mystic Perfections
56. Possessing Inconceivable Potencies
57. His Body Generates Innumerable Universes
58. The Original Source of All Incarnations
59. Gives Salvation to the Enemies He Kills
60. Attractor of Liberated Souls
61. Performer of Wonderful Activities
62. Always is Surrounded by Loving Devotees
63. Attractive Flute
64. Has Unrivalled Excellence of Beauty in the Creation

MAHA - GREAT - BHARAT

Bharat, later called India, was at the peak of its progress in every field during the time of Mahabharat. In this Golden Age, arts and sciences were so well developed that they can stand up to the latest advances of the 21st Century. The oldest written text, the Vedas, are the encyclopedia of ancient Indian knowledge, arts and science. Even UNESCO has acknowledged that the Vedas are the ultimate source of knowledge.

ARCHITECTURE

The aesthetic temples and grand palaces show the high level of architecture and building construction based on Vastu Shastra. Residential and commercial buildings were constructed to meet all purposes of life with proper consideration for hygiene and all comforts. Shrimad Bhagavatam mentions Narada Rishi saying architects carried out perfect city and town planning. Shrimad Bhagavatam (1-11-14) reveals that renowned architect, Viswakarma, created Dwarka (now in Gujarat) at short notice for the Supreme Lord Krishna. It was a big city with high-ways, sub-ways, by-lanes, markets, public meeting places, parks, gardens and lakes.

ASTRONOMY

A detailed knowledge of the the sun, the moon, the planets, the stars, including the Pole Star or Dhruva, and earth planet was well developed and used for different purposes. The ancient texts divide this universe into 14 divisions of planetary systems, calculated from earthly planetary systems called Bhurloka. Six planetary systems exist in the upper region: Bhuvar loka, Svar loka, Mahar loka, Jana loka, Tapa loka and Satya loka. Seven planetary systems exist in the lower regions of Bhur loka: Atala, Vitala, Sutala, Tala tala, Maha tala, Rasa tala and Patala. Distances between the earth and the sun, moon and different planets was precisely calculated. This knowledge of astronomy was used in astrology and navigation.

AIRPLANES

Shrimad Bhagavatam (7-10-54 and 55) states that the Maya danava constructed invisible airplane known as Tripura which was made of gold, silver, iron and of uncommon materials.

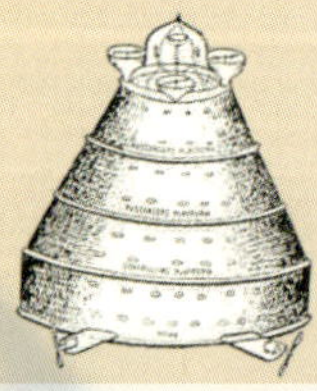

ARTS

Music and dancing were performed by 'gandharvas' and 'apsaras' respectively. The roots of classical Indian music and dance are firmly in the Vedas. Dedicated to the Gods, singing and dancing were a divine experience. Sculpture and painting were also well developed as seen in the temples and palaces.

MAHA - GREAT - BHARAT

ATOMIC SCIENCES

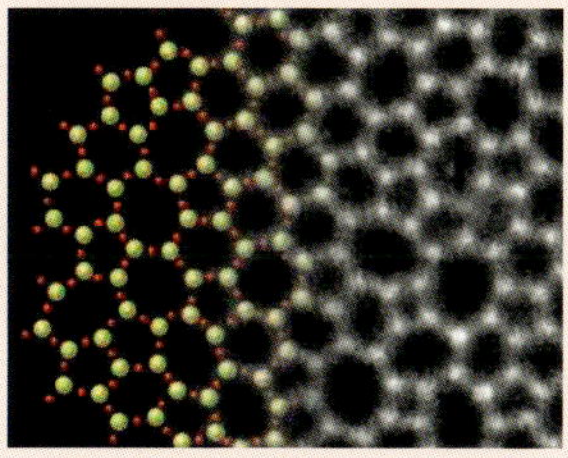

The description of the atom in the Srimad Bhagavatam is almost the same as the modern science. In modern science, the atom is considered as the ultimate indivisible particle of which the universe is composed. Srimad Bhagavatam defines it exactly: "The material manifestation's ultimate particle, which is indivisible and not formed into a body, is called the atom. It exists always as an invisible identity, even after the dissolution of all forms. The material body is but a combination of such atoms, but it is misunderstood by the common man." (3-11-1) "Atoms are the ultimate state of the manifest universe. When they stay in their own forms without forming different bodies, they are called the unlimited oneness. There are certainly different bodies in physical forms, but the atoms themselves form the complete manifestation." (3-11-2).

The atom is described as an invisible particle, but when six such atoms combine together, they are called a trasarenu, and this is visible in the sunshine pouring through the holes of a window screen. The time needed for integration of three trasarenu is a truti.

COSMOLOGY

The universe is in the grip of a kind of anti-gravity effect called "dark energy", according to National Aeronautic Space Administration (NASA) of USA probe in 2001. In Sanskrit, 'tamah' means darkness. Lord Krishna refers to this energy as 'Mohini Prakriti', or the illusory nature by which the cosmic creation takes place. Therefore, Lord Krishna's material energy is the dark energy. The NASA probe revealed that the 'dark energy', made of completely unknown matter, is the most powerful driving force in the expansion of the cosmos. Lord Krishna says that the three forms of this energy - goodness, passion and ignorance - influence all living beings to perform their actions helplessly. In the Gita, the Lord asserts that this dark energy is very powerful and hence insurmountable. The NASA probe compelled the scientists to conclude that all the constituents of the universe originated from the same point and that all the material that makes up everything in the universe was once contained within a single point until it was released in the Big Bang eventually coalescing to form stars, planets and you and me. According to Vedic cosmology, Lord Krishna is the creator of cosmic manifestations as revealed by him in the Gita.

MAHA - GREAT - BHARAT

ECONOMICS

Kautilya's treatise 'Arthashastra' covers most modern concepts of economics for production, distribution, consumption, taxation, monetary policy and even governance since the ancient, agrarian economy was well developed. With abundant production of food, forest products and minerals, the economy's production, distribution and consumption systems were fully developed and operational.

EDUCATION

Basic education was available for all four classes of the society, proficiency in Vedic knowledge was considered as the real education. Only the Brahmanas had access to the Vedas because they lived in sattva, the mode of goodness. Unless one is situated in sattvic mode, it is impossible to grasp the intrinsic purports of Vedic statements. An educated person in this era was one who can see the individual spirit soul or jivatma and the supreme spirit soul or paramatma in every living being, not attaching importance to the physical body. In other words, in Vedic Civilization one was considered educated if one possessed the knowledge of one's spiritual identity that is different from bodily identification.

EMBRYOLOGY

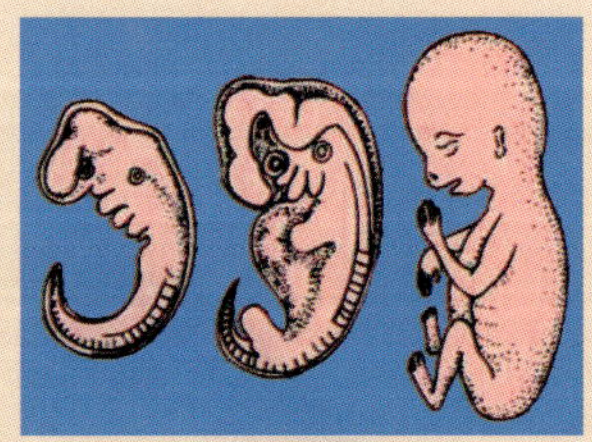

The Shrimad Bhagavatam (3-31-2,3,4,10) explains the gradual development of the embryo up to the time leading to delivery. On the first night, the sperm and ovum mix; on the fifth night, the mixture ferments into a bubble; on the tenth night, it develops into a form like a plum; and then, it gradually turns into a lump of flesh or an egg, as the case may be. (3-31-2). In the course of a month, a head is formed, and at the end of two months the hands, feet and other limbs take shape. By the end of three months, the nail, fingers, toes, body hair, bones and skin appear, as do the organs and the other apertures in the body, the eyes, nostrils, ears, mouth and anus. (3-31-3).

Within four months from the date of conception, the seven essential ingredients of the body, chyle, blood, flesh, fat, bone, marrow and semen, take shape. At the end of five months, hunger and thirst make themselves felt, and at the end of six months, the fetus, enclosed by the amnion, begins to move on the right side of the abdomen. (3-31-4). Thus endowed with the development of consciousness from the seventh month after his conception, the child is tossed downward by the airs that press the embryo during the weeks preceding delivery. (3-31-10)

MAHA - GREAT - BHARAT

MATHEMATICS

The zero, the decimal system, algebra, geometry, trigonometry, quadratic equations and many other concepts originated in Vedic mathematics known for precision and accuracy in calculations. This is best illustrated by the method by which time is measured. The modern terms for Vedic time segments are:

One truti	*8/13,500*	*Second*	*One laghu*	*2 minutes*
One vedha	*8/135*	*Second*	*One danda*	*30 minutes*
One lava	*8/45*	*Second*	*One prahara*	*3 hours*
One nimesa	*8/15*	*Second*	*One day*	*12 hours*
One ksana	*8/5*	*Second*	*One night*	*12 hours*
One kastha	*8*	*Seconds*	*One paksa*	*15 days (Fortnight)*

Two pakhsas comprise one month, and twelve months comprise one calendar year, or one full orbit of the sun. There are four millenniums or yugas: Satya, Treta, Dwapara and Kali. The last one is the present millennium. Each millennium lasts for: Satya for 1,728,000 years, Treta for 1,296,000 years, Dwapara for 864,000 years and Kali for 432,000 years; one cycle of four yugas for 4,320,000 years.

MEDICINE AND HEALTH

One of the branches of the Vedas, Ayurveda, contains detailed knowledge about the science of health. Human anatomy, physiology, metabolism, genetics and immunity were well known and surgery was practised with over 125 instruments and anesthesia. The qualities of spices and forest products were harnessed for preventive medicine while the science of yoga was practised for physical, mental and spiritual progress.

NUCLEAR MISSILES

The battle of Kurukshetra mentions nuclear missiles such as Varuneya and Agneya but the most devastating among them, of course is Brahmastra, completely invincible. These missiles were launched and withdrawn by some specific mantra vibrations and therefore, all soldiers did not have access to them because it required certain eligibility and special skills among the leaders of the warriors.

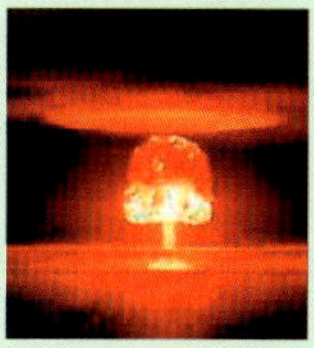

MAHA - GREAT - BHARAT

POLITICAL ADMINISTRATION

During the Mahabharata era, only Kshatriyas (the warrior class) managed political administration, diplomacy and warfare. This is based on their natural qualities of 'heroism, power, determination, resourcefulness, courage in battle, generosity and leadership' as outlined by the Supreme Lord Krishna in the Gita (18/43). They were also properly trained in administrative affairs from their early age. Since Kshatriyas are predominantly influenced by raja guna, mode of passion, they are empowered to rule, organise and lead people in virtuous living.

Monarchy was the political system in Vedic civilization. This is because a Kshatriya emperor is directly the representative of the Supreme Lord Krishna and is supposed to be appointed by Him to look after the Lord's interests on this planet as confirmed in Shrimad Bhagavatam (4-21-22 and 23): "By the grace of the Supreme Lord I have been appointed the king of this planet, and I carry the scepter to rule the citizens, protect them from all danger and give them employment according to their respective positions in the social order established by Vedic injunction."

To ensure flawless administration, the Kshatriya kings always diligently followed instructions and advice of qualified ministerial board of Brahmanas of spotless character. They advised the king on all matters based on guidelines provided in religious scriptures like Manu Samhita and other Dharma Shastras of the Saint Parasara. The Brahmanas were qualified as advisers because their nature was predominantly Sattvik, the material mode of goodness superior to the nature of the kings.

PHYSICAL SCIENCES

The civilisation had detailed knowledge of physics, chemistry, biology that includes the theory of evolution with a total of 8,400,000 species within the universe as 9,00,000 aquatic creatures, 20,00,000 plants, trees and creepers, 11,00,000 insects and reptiles, 10,00,000 birds, 30,00,000 mammals and 4,00,000 humans.

SOCIAL STRUCTURE

Society was classified according to the institution of Varna-Ashrama that provided the opportunity to realise one's potential and make spiritual progress. The Supreme Lord Krishna says in Gita (4/13) that the four divisions of human society are created by him, on the basis of one's quality or qualification and the activity one performs. To lead a healthy and purposeful life, one must possess a head, two hands, a stomach and two legs. In this system, the head means Brahmanas, the intellectual class; the hands mean Kshatriyas, the administrative class; the stomach represents Vaishyas, the mercantile class; and the legs represent Shudras, the labour class. Hence, for a society to run smoothly, all the four classes are needed. But with the advent of the modern age or Kaliyuga, this system became distorted as classification was carried out merely on the basis of birth which is totally opposed to the principles in the Gita.

ARMY POWER IN THE WAR OF KURUKSHKETRA

WEAPONS

In addition to the normal weapons of war of those days like daggers, swords and shields, tridents, battle axes, bows and arrows, maces, among others; there were special weapons, like whirling missiles, granted by gods to select warriors. Some famous missiles were: Brahmshastra given to Arjun, Shakti shastra given o Karan, Naga Astra that could create a huge serpant, Bhaggav Astra and missiles that could create fierce storms, douse water, spread fire, release poisonous gases among other deadly devices to wipe out tens of thousands of soldiers with a single missile.

CHARIOTS

The chariots were filled with quivers of arrows, javelins, long handled spears, barbed darts, heavy maces, wooden and metal clubs, long ropes, pots filled with snakes, clubs with iron spikes, swords, short and long bows, battle axes and forked lances. Each chariot was yoked with minimum four horses of the top breeds. Each chariot had six men - four warriors, a driver and a reserve driver. Chariots were like a town surrounded by elephants like the walls of a town. The chariots were like tanks of a modern army.

ELEPHANTS

On the back of each elephant, there were seven warriors. Two among them with hooks, two were excellent bowmen, two swordsmen and one with a lance and a trident. Around each chariot, there were ten elephants. Each elephant was assisted by ten horses and ten infantry men guarded each horse. Around each horseman seven foot soldiers were attached.
There were also huge formations of elephants and horses to tackle exigencies.

ARMY

Kaurava's army had eleven Akshauhinis or Divisions and Pandavas had seven. An Akshauhini – A Division of troops consisting of:

1) Chariots 21,780 each with four warriors, a driver and a reserve driver - thus six men per chariot - total men 21780 x 6 = 130,680.
2) Elephants 21, 780 - each with 7 warriors - 21,780 x 7 = 152,460.
3) Horses 65, 150 - one horseman on each animal = 65,150.
4) Soldiers 1, 09, 350.

Total Manpower per Division = 457,640.

Pandavas - Seven divisions = 3,203,480.
Kauravas - Eleven Divisions = 5,034,040.
Total Army Power = 8,237,520.

Source: Mahabharata by Shriji Dasa, Published by Rasbihari Lal & Sons, Lio Bazaar, Vrindaban - 281121, UP.

ARMY POWER IN THE WAR OF KURUKSHKETRA

KURUKSHETRA WAR

All the warriors were entirely wiped out within 18 days, leaving the Supreme Lord Krishna, Satyaki and five Pandavas alive on the Pandava side. Kripacharya,Kritavarma and Ashwathama remained alive on the Kaurava side.

ANCIENT WORLD'S TOP ARMIES

Persian Army:

Xerxes I, Emperor of Persia, prepared for four years for years to continue the Persian war against Greece started by his father, Darius. In 481 B.C., the Persian army and navy arrived in Asia Minor. Greek historian Herodotus calculated the total at 2.6 million. He added that this number needs to be nearly doubled to account for support troops, and thus the whole force numbered 5,283,220 men.

Alexander The Great:

The Greek army under Alexander never exceeded 80,000 and yet it crossed into Asia Minor into India and into Egypt on its return where Alexander died in Alexandria.

Genghis Khan:

His Mongol army never numbered more than 100,000 warriors, yet it subjugated more lands and people in twenty-five years than the Romans conquered in four hundred.

Thutmose III:

Egypt's greatest warrior pharaoh, fought 17 campaigns abroad and was victorious in all of them to establish his empire deep into Asia. His first-rate professional army had about a quarter of a million soldiers that put Egypt on its pinnacle as a military power.

MODERN WORLD'S TOP ARMIES

Currently, the world's top ten armies total 6,680,000. Krurkshetra had more soldiers totaling 8,237,520 than the current total of the world's top ten armies at 6,680,000.

MODERN ARMY

A divisionis a large military unit usually consisting of between ten to fifteen thousand soldiers but it can go up to thirty thousand

Top Ten Countries with the Largest Armies

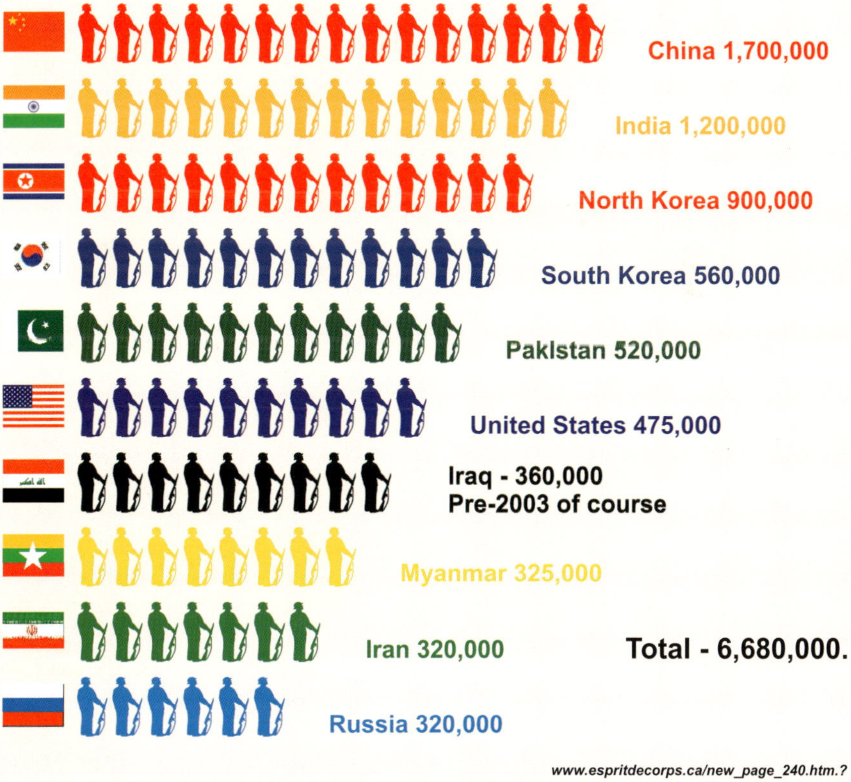

www.espritdecorps.ca/new_page_240.htm.?

WORLD'S TOP TEN COUNTRIES WITH LARGE ARMIES

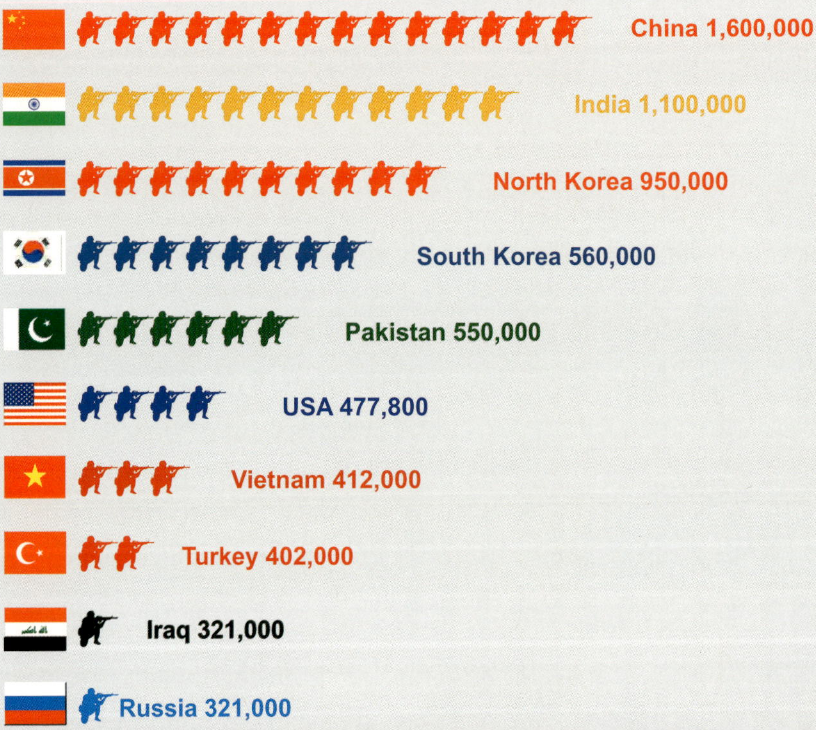

Source: World's Largest Army, Largest Army in the World

Notes:

China deploys the world's largest ground force, currently totaling some 1.6 million personnel, or about 70% of the total manpower of 2.3 million in 2005. The reserve component has about 1.2–1.5 million personnel.

India With more than 1,130,000 soldiers in active service and about 1,800,000 reserve troops, the Indian Army is the world's second largest.

United States A division in the US Army typically consists of 10,000 to 20,000 soldiers commanded by a Major General. The United States Army currently has ten active divisions: The United States Army also consists of eight Divisions within the National Guard. The US Marine Corps has a further three active divisions and one reserve division.

Managing Methods:
Commerical or Krishna Consciousness?

Corporate Operations	Commercial Considerations	Krishna Consciousness
Profits	Maximise for owners	Reasonable for owners and for spreading Krishna's message
Pricing	For highest returns	Within consumer's affordable range (because quality products are always high-priced)
Production	Extreme cost cutting at expense of quality	Modest cost sutting to offer quality and value
Distribution	For highest returns	For quality and value
Marketing	False exaggerated claims	True benefits
Staffing	Lowest wages/salaries Exploitation	Following full legal norms, Fair dealings
Research & Development	Minimum Illegally using competitors' results	Original efforts for original breakthroughs
Corporate Strategy	Fair or unfair practices for maximum profits	Fair practices for reasonable profits
Promotional/ Publicity	False/exaggerated highlights of product features.	offering genuine information
After-Sales Service	Tricky and complicated guarantee	Properly spelt out consumer friendly assurances

ROCK STEADY AND DEVOTIONAL DANCING

MODERN MANAGEMENT

21ST CENTURY MANAGEMENT

At the beginning of the 21th century,
business management came to consist of six separate branches:

ALL THREE PATHS CONVERGE IN ONE

Bhakti Yoga
Loving, Devotional Service to Lord Krishna

Karma Yoga	Jnana Yoga	Dhyana Yoga
Disclipined Physical Action to Lord Krishna	Intellectual Persuit Spiritual Quest for Lord Krishna	Meditation Concentration on Lord Krishna

THE VARNA OR CASTE SYSTEM

Varna is the system of professional hierarchy as per the laws of Manu. Originally, it is based on natural aptitude and ability for work after their education and training. Later, it became a standard system for classifying the people according to their birth.

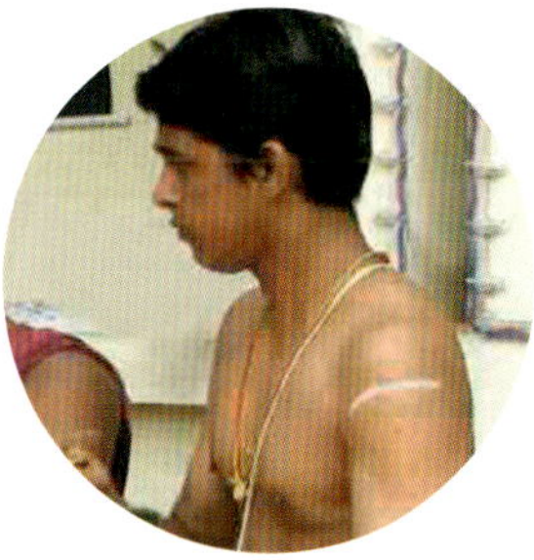

BRAHMANAS

Intellectuals, Visionaries, Advisors, Gurus, Teachers, Priests.

Main Qualities

Knowledge, Wisdom, Control of the Mind and the Five Senses, Mercy, Truthfulness Forgiveness, Contentment and Complete Surrender to God.

Main Duties

Educating with Spiritual Guidance Determining the Values and Vision of the Society, Advising and Guiding the Kshatriyas, Accepting Charity, Never Accepting Paid Employment.

KSHATRIYAS

Warriors, Rulers and Administrators.

Main Qualities

Brave, Fearless, Chivalrous, Generous, Truthful, Determined and Resourceful.

Main Duties

Protecting Citizens, Ruling with Justice, Uncompromising with Crime and Lawlessness, Never Refusing a Challenge, Following the Advice and Guidance of Brahamanas.

VAISHYAS

Farmers, Merchants, Business Persons

Main Qualities

Hard Working, Trading Ethically, Devoted to Gurus and Lord Vishnu and Faithful to the Scriptures.

Main Duties

Farming, Trading, Creating Wealth and Prosperity, Employing Workers with Adequate Compensation, Protecting Nature, Especially Cows.

SHUDRAS

Artisans, Workers, Servants

Main Qualities

Obedient, Truthful in All Dealings, Following the Advice of Brahamanas, Kshatriyas and Vaishyas.

Main Duties

Serving Brahamanas, Kshatriyas and Vaishyas Faithfully, Following Moral and Religious Principles to Serve the Society.

Surrender to the Supreme Lord: *Arjuna said: My dear Kṛṣṇa, O Infallible One, my illusion is now gone. I have regained my memory by Your mercy. I am now firm and free from doubt and am prepared to act according to Your instructions. (Gita Ch. 18.73)*

Chapter 1

The Centre of All Businesses

Presiding over the strategic meetings of the Pandavas, the Supreme Lord Shri Krishna implements almost all the principles of modern management—just like any CEO of a modern multi-national. If one imagines a modern boardroom with the Supreme Lord Krishna at the head of the table and the five Pandavas as directors of operations for different areas, one can immediately perceive the close similarities with modern management practices.

Like all committed company directors, the Pandavas have complete trust, loyalty and confidence in their CEO. In fact, they are totally surrendered to him. As the meeting proceeds, Yudishthira, the eldest Pandava, who always follows the path of truth and righteousness, provides the strategic options. Next, the great warrior Bhima, who is renowned for his great strength and fighting skills, provides inputs towards army capabilities and performance. The third eldest, Arjuna, who is virtually the Commander-in-Chief, explains the state of the battle and plans the next moves. The fourth Pandava Nakul, a master horse rider, informs about the state and preparedness of the cavalry. The youngest, Sahdev, who came from the God of Medicine, outlines the medical and health facilities for the army. As he is also known to be the most intelligent of the five, in diplomacy and political manoueuvres, monitors all intelligence about both the armed forces.

As the war strategy is discussed with inputs from all five Pandavas on the state of the conflict, the Supreme Lord Sri Krishna leads from the front on all issues and decisions based on the colossal scale of operations. Mass production is the basic foundation for this humongous undertaking. The two armies consist of 18 '*akshouhinis*' or divisions numbering 8.2 million armed forces equipped with uniforms and weapons, food and accommodation, medical and transport services. The mass production of such high-quality, well-designed products and services proves that this ancient civilization had developed in all fields of excellence. The administration of such a gigantic operation calls for very high management skills. In modern management terms, this means research and development, acquisition, storage, distribution, maintenance and transport of all equipment and consumables. Record-keeping for all the manpower and equipment involves creating, maintaining and updating massive databases. Thus, all decisions have to be based on pragmatic management decisions—no different from modern management practices.

This raises a fundamental question: the Supreme Lord Sri Krishna, leading the five Pandavas, is fighting for the victory of the truth; so how can his teachings in the *Gita* be applied when it urges to strive without hankering for results? Similarly, how can these management principles of the Supreme Lord Krishna be applied to the corporate world today where profit is the first priority?

If an entire organization becomes conscious of the teachings of the Supreme Lord Krishna, only then will the teachings in the *Gita* apply. If the corporation as a whole does not believe in the Supreme Lord Krishna or God Consciousness, then the *Gita* becomes irrelevant. Anybody claiming or propagating that a corporate body can be profiteering and can at the same time apply the *Gita's* teachings and principles, is actually desecrating religion. This is because an organization becomes useless when it, in its entirety, is not into Krishna Consciousness, as all its operations and functions cannot be performed or operated under those principles. The basic principles of the *Gita* have to be accepted because in the *Gita*, the Supreme Lord Krishna has provided many concessions even for modern times. For example, he says, "First is Kamya *karma* or furtive activities which means performing action with a desire for enjoying results according to socio-religious structure. Next comes *Nishkama karma* or activity without hankering for enjoying results and offering them to the Supreme Lord Krishna. By such adherence, one can gradually advance spiritually also while performing secular duties."

In the corporate sector or in any marketing or industrial organization, one cannot operate without expecting positive results. It has to be "result-oriented". In a marketing organization, the chief executive has to achieve, if not exceed, quarterly, half-yearly and annual targets.

The sales force has to sell accordingly, based on 'a journey cycle form' which is completed regularly. Thus, given targets have to be achieved. How can one not hanker for results? The hankering is not wrong. Action produces results and the results have to be offered to the Supreme Lord Krishna. This is called *Karma Arpanam.* Once this is understood and implemented, all the rest will fit in properly. A corporate or a profit-oriented organization is not a charitable organization. Profit is essential. But a certain percentage of profits, for running the organization, is needed, while the rest should be spent in spreading the Supreme Lord Krishna's message. Of course, the owners or the shareholders may not agree. That is why it is necessary that all of them, and the entire organization, have to be into Krishna Consciousness, so that they can impress the same upon the shareholders.

Who is Qualified to Lead?

At first sight, it may not look possible or realistic. A Managing Director (MD) or a Chief Executive Officer (CEO) must have the vision to be into Krishna Consciousness and manage the organization. Not only the MD or the CEO but all heads of all departments and business executives have to be into Krishna Consciousness. Unless one is a sinless person, one is not qualified to lead an organization. How can a sinful person lead? It goes, "*Andha yatha andhaiva upaniyamanah.*" It is like one blind person leading another. In other words, the head of the organization should be sinless, and only then can he guide the corporation.

But major corporations or multi-national organizations (MNCs) of today's world are not headed by so-called sinless persons, and yet they are successful and making billions of dollars' worth of profits. While this is true, one can also see the consequences of their actions. MNCs have ravaged the earth of its resources and created environmental hazards and destruction. MNCs have cheated millions of their hard-earned savings while their directors have decamped with huge sums. And the latest Global Financial Crisis of 2008 has shown how greedy company executives have brought down the global financial system.

Look at the fourth richest man in the world: Warren Buffet. At the age of 73, he gave away millions of dollars to charity. Up to the age of 73, he struggled a great deal to earn those billions and ultimately he thought that it was all useless. He lives a very simple life without the luxuries and frills of billionaires. This shows that the mere accumulation of money is not the source of happiness. Had he been a Krishna Conscious person, he would have given up those results to the Supreme Lord Krishna in a systematic manner which would have helped him as well as the nation or whichever country he is in. There is nothing wrong in making profits. But the profits should be spent in spreading the Supreme Lord Krishna's message. If that can be done, an organization's prosperity will be perfect, otherwise we will see sins being committed and sinfulness increasing everywhere.

Again, why is the second richest man in the world, Bill Gates, giving huge amounts to charity? Because that is the right way. He may not be into Krishna Consciousness, but he has realised that one cannot hoard profits for one's personal enjoyment. There is a limit. So, he is giving his money to charity. In an organization, a good percentage of the profits should be earmarked for reinvestment or diversification, but the rest should be spent in spreading the Supreme Lord Krishna's message. The problem with today's CEOs is that every one of them wants to become one of the top billionaires of the world.

Moreover, the shareholders want more and more, and they keep on pushing the other executives to make more profits. The results have been tragically highlighted in the latest Global Financial Crisis report. The right-minded executives have to convince the shareholders that by managing these corporations to maximise profits at the expense of everything else, we end up with disastrous results—both for the economy and the environment.

Five years after this Global Financial Crisis, the economy of the United States and Britain have not recovered. Western Europe has been reeling under severe unemployment and meagre economic, if not flat, growth. This worldwide downturn had a domino effect on developing countries, including the high-growth economies of China and India, which were also impacted by the same slide. Millions of jobs have been lost and millions of companies have closed down causing untold suffering to people. Low economic activity, low incomes for individuals and companies, translates to low tax collection while the governments have to spend more to revive their economies. Known as 'stimulus spending', this expenditure has ballooned government deficits.

The *Gita's* teachings don't apply at the national level in such an environment. You cannot implement the *Gita's* principles in a Godless organization. The Supreme Lord Krishna told Arjuna in the Gita (4/2), "*Evam Parampara praptam imam Rajarishayo viduh,*" which means that the saintly kings understood the supreme science of the *Gita* through the chain of disciples' succession.

The word "*rajarshi*" means all the great kings like Yuddhishtra, Parikshit, Dilip or Raghu, who were all great administrators and ruled the entire earth. But they were into Krishna Consciousness and applied the *Gita's* principles. The ruler of the entire earth during the Vedic times, Maharaja Ambarisha, was devoted to the Supreme Lord Krishna. As a ruler, he had to collect taxes but these taxes were collected like the sun absorbing water and giving it back in the form of rains at the appropriate time. The taxes collected were spent for the welfare of the people. Everything was done equitably in the interest of the people.

The Centre of All Activities

So the Supreme Lord Krishna must be the centre of all activities or there will be chaos. We need to either be prepared for sinning and suffering or act according to the *Gita's* principles and live happily. For example, if a CEO is not a sinless man, he immediately becomes a corrupt man, who achieves everything in his life only through corrupt means. It is said, "*Yasyasti bhagavati bhaktir akancana sarva gunaih tatra samasate surah*," meaning that one who is a devotee of Lord Hari attracts all demigods of good qualities to come and reside in his body. He exhibits excellent transcendental behaviour at all times.

For example, if a CEO is Krishna conscious, he will not produce and sell shoddy goods as quality goods; he will not destroy natural resources to make short-term profits; he will not prepare false accounts; or participate in similar unethical practices like paying bribes to get approvals or contracts. He will follow all the legal requirements in manufacturing, marketing, distribution, staff and public relations, in fact, in managing his company, and charge a fair price that provides value for money. Moreover, he will be conscious of his social obligations towards his community at large and those who are less fortunate in his community and country. On top of it all, he will earmark a good percentage of his company's profits for spreading the Supreme Lord Krishna's message for the spiritual uplift of the people he serves.

We should understand that we must perform all our activities to ensure that our Lord is satisfied with our actions. We seem to be serving negative forces like greed and envy. If the Lord is not satisfied by our actions, then we cannot be satisfied. That is why today nobody is satisfied—be it the rich or the poor, literate or illiterate.

Becoming Krishna conscious can prevent an organization from getting a bad reputation. This is because the world is full of, and dominated by, sinful people. The so-called successful people, including many CEOs who have been exposed and disgraced, are those who indulge in regular and heavy drinking, gambling and immoral sex. But if one has been trained in Krishna Consciousness, he or she will not resort to all these immoral activities. CEOs can, of course, enjoy the material world, but in a regulated way. Then they set an example for all their employees, be it in a small company or a major corporation, which reflects the personality and qualities of its top management. This moral behaviour percolates from the top to the bottom. If I am a drunkard, I will tell my assistant to join me for a drink. The employee might then assume that by bribing this man with imported whisky, he can get a promotion. Thus, it is very important for the top management should be clean.

Vedic literature describes the four major sins as "*Dyutam panam striyah soona yatra adharmah chaturvidhah*"— gambling, intoxication, prostitution and eating animal flesh. Gambling includes all speculative activities including betting on racehorses, playing cards, chess, lottery, video games as well as some investments in the stock market. Intoxicants include tea, coffee, all alcoholic drinks, drugs, chewing betel leaves and betel nuts as well as smoking cigarettes and consumption of tobacco including snuff. Prostitution covers all kinds of illegitimate physical union for carnal enjoyment other than that permitted by Vedic scriptural codes in terms of a man-woman physical relationship sanctified through marriage in a civilized human society. Animal flesh means the flesh of all land-based and water-based animals as well as birds. This also includes eggs. These four vices uproot the very moral and ethical foundation of human society. These are considered sins for many reasons.

The Four Pitfalls

Firstly, those who eat animal flesh tend to become merciless in their dealings with other human beings and show violent reactions. Non-vegetarians lack compassion. It is said, "You are what you eat," and therefore, a non-vegetarian gradually develops animalistic propensities. The eighteenth-century German philosopher Immanuel Kant believed that cruelty to animals should be abjured if not for no other reason than that "Such brutality leads to a violent mentality that is then likely to be directed at one's own fellow man."[1] The renowned mathematician Pythagoras substantiates this saying: "As long as men massacre animals, they will kill each other."

Secondly, those who are addicted to intoxicants in one form or the other are, to a larger or lesser extent, bound to behave in an irresponsible way, ruining their own and their family members' lives. Corporates host cocktails and dinners where liquour and meat are normally served. This is reflected in their work as corporate executives and leads to absenteeism, irrational behaviour and illogical decisions.

Thirdly, the persons who regularly indulge in illicit relationships outside marriage will treat others, including their elders, with irreverence as well as see the members of the opposite sex merely as the objects of sense stimuli and nothing more. Promiscuous men and women are invariably bereft of all moral codes and ethics. Sexual harassment at work has become a major problem in most countries and has emerged in the public domain even in developing countries like India in recent years. The bosses exploit their position to sexually harass their junior women employees—a practice going on for many decades but now exposed in public view as women fight for their rights under stringent new laws.

Fourthly, gamblers always resort to falsehood, intoxicants and force people to give up all austerity. The man and the woman for whom gambling, in any form, is irresistible, will lose faith in earning a livelihood through honest means and take excessive and unwarranted risks in personal and corporate affairs. Thus, they can ruin their lives and their companies, and still their demand for money for gambling will not be satisfied.

---

[1] Page 161 of *The Ideas of Immanuel Kant* by Bertrand Schulman, New Jersey: Philosophical Publishing, 1984.

Many believe that business is a gamble. But it is not so if performed on religious principles. These days business means both buyers and sellers consciously agreeing to cheat each other. In the Vedic era, the Vaishyas, the merchant community, were religious. Hence, they operated on a minimum profit basis. They financially helped those engaged in preaching activities of God consciousness. In this way, they were spending the money from their profits.

It can be argued that in the Vedic times, during the years of the *Mahabharata*, the kings drank liquour, ate meat, gambled and indulged in illicit sex during some notable incidents such as the gambling sessions between the Kauravas and the Pandavas; the hunting of animals was followed by royal feasts, babies were born out of wedlock as in the case of Karna. It is important to remember that these activities were permitted to Kshatriyas to maintain their physical prowess, bravery and valour under the Vedic system but not to other three castes.

The Kshatriyas drank only on special occasions a liquor by the name "varuni", a preparation of rice.. They also ate meat of animals offered in Vedic fire sacrifices conducted by Brahmin priests of unblemished character. Moreover, the spirit soul, the real living being of the animal thus sacrificed, was immediately promoted to heavenly planets for more refined enjoyment.

Except for the misbehaviour of some sinful Kshatriyas, generally there were no incidents involving illicit sex. It is because the Kshatriya kings were allowed to marry many women. All such married wives were taken care of by the kings in all respects except that the sons born of such wives could not stake claims to a king's throne after his demise. Only the sons of the chief among the queens had the natural prerogative to succeed as king.

As for the birth of Karna, it was a result of his mother Kunti's attempt to test the efficacy of the boon she received from the sage Durvasa. It was out of curiosity and not due to wanton, lustful behaviour. Moreover, the exalted and empowered Sun God's momentary association with Kunti did not however result in defilement as would have been in the case of ordinary human beings.

According to the regulative principles of the Varna- Ashrama (socio-religious) system, Kshatriyas were obliged to accept invitations to both gambling as well as dual combats. They were not supposed to refuse. That is why even the virtuous King Yudishthira accepted the invitation from the Kauravas for the game of dice.

The Norm: Unethical Practices

Unethical practices, cheating and lying have become the norm in today's business world. Plenty of examples are found every day: shoddy products advertised as top-quality products, services sold with false promises, contracts not fulfilled, after-sales service denied, and so on. In real estate, the developers collect high amounts in advance payments for premises not delivered on time or supplied with shoddy construction.

In the *Gita*, the Supreme Lord Krishna himself tells lies to promote goodness. But we cannot compare the Supreme Lord Krishna's actions to our unwarranted practices. The Supreme Lord Sri Krishna is transcendental. He is beyond all principles—good or bad, moral or immoral. He is not covered by material injunctions or influenced by physical nature. He is above all these things. This is mentioned in the *Gita*. His birth and activities are transcendental. The Supreme Lord Krishna's strategy was to defeat non-religious activities by non-religious ways. On the spiritual level, there is no duality. There is no piety or impiety. Impiety is also piety here. That is the difference between our actions and those of the Supreme Lord Krishna. We cannot promote cheating or sins. If a CEO is a sinless person, he allots duties to subordinates according to their nature, like in the *varnasrama* system instituted by the Supreme Lord Krishna and as explained in the *Gita*.

In international operations, the same principles apply because the operators in both domestic and global markets have the same mindset of physical enjoyment and self-aggrandizement. This needs to be rectified. The Supreme Lord Krishna's principles are for universal application. This is totally spiritual. In the *Gita*, the Supreme Lord Krishna says, "If you want to operate on the material platform, then you operate on my behalf." It is as in the case of demi-god Brahma. The Supreme Lord Krishna in the form of Lord Vishnu created the basic ingredients of this Universe. It is Brahma who acted as the secondary creator by creating all the other details within. He also created all the embodied living beings of various species. Although this cosmic construction by the Engineer Brahma is a total material activity, he performed this action on behalf of, and for the pleasure of, the Supreme Lord Krishna. The CEO should bear in mind: "I am handling the property of the Supreme Lord Krishna on His behalf." He should have that vision while operating, only then will his way of operation be perfect. These principles also apply to competition, corporate wars, mergers and acquisitions.

It is very clearly said in the *Gita* that the material world is full of miseries (*dukhalayam*) and it is temporary (*ashashvatham*). These are two drawbacks of this material world which the Supreme Lord Krishna himself admits in the *Bhagavad Gita* (8:16):

Mam upetya punar janma duhkhalayam asasvatam
Napnuvanti mahatmanah samsuddhim paramam gatah

He himself points out that this material existence is full of miseries. Nobody can be happy here; *ashashvatam*—everything is temporary here.

Guiding the CEOs

So how will the Supreme Lord Krishna guide CEOs to operate in this sinful, miserable world? There is no question that they should operate for selfish ends. He says, *Kamya karma*, that is out of sheer addiction over the past few lives, you are forced, indeed you are bound, and you are compelled to do some activity while desiring to enjoy the results of those activities. This is your addiction. This addiction has to be broken. But that's not possible overnight. There are two words technically: "*Kartritva*" *and* "*Bhogtritva*". *Kartritva* is action and *Bhogtritva* is enjoyment. So the Supreme Lord Krishna says, "Due to your addiction, initially, you give up the *bhogtritva* or enjoyment; keep performing your activity, your *kratritva* and offer the results to Me." Ultimately what sense does it make to perform an activity to ultimately give up the results? So, you will decide: "Let me not perform the activity at all." Then you direct all your energies to perform only those activities for the satisfaction of the Supreme Lord Krishna, exactly like Arjuna who fought for the exclusive satisfaction of the Lord without any consideration for victory or defeat. But the Pandavas did win by the mercy of the Lord ultimately.

> *Yajnarthat karmano n'yatra loko'yam karma-bandhanah*
> *Tad-artham karma kaunteya mukta-sangah samacara*
> *(Bhagavad Gita 3:9)*

Work done as a sacrifice for Viu has to be performed; otherwise work causes bondage in this material world. Therefore, O son of Kunt, perform your prescribed duties for His satisfaction, and in that way you will always remain free from bondage.

That realization will come. The preliminary step is giving up the result without enjoyment and gradually surrendering to the Lord.

The most important action for an executive is decision-making. He/she has to take decisions all the time. This teaching in the *Gita* helps him/her to take the right decision. Unless he/she is trained as the devotee of the Lord, he/she cannot take the right decision. In the major universities around the world, there is a department to study almost every discipline. But there is no department to study about the soul. But just saying there is no such department is not good enough. It is better to create this department.

If you want to implement the *Bhagavad Gita's* principles, you should train your subordinates as per the *Gita's* teachings. It is like an apprenticeship of three years for fresh graduate engineers and after successful completion of the training period, these engineers are employed at a certain grade, given designations and a high salary. So when you sign up young new employees with degrees like B Tech, MBA, or just fresh graduates, make them pure devotees of Krishna to learn the principles of the *Gita*, so that they take morally right decisions. Otherwise, their decision-making will be on a trial-and-error basis. Their decisions will not always yield desired results. Sometimes because of foolish decisions made a CEO may even lose his job. Arjuna, a superb *kshatriya*, an expert in warfare, became bewildered and admitted that he was not able to take a decision whether to fight or not. After understanding the principles of Krishna Consciousness, he said, "*Karishye vachanam tava*,"(I shall do exactly as per your instructions.). Simply proclaiming that you can implement the *Gita's* principles in the corporate world is not enough. They have to be put into action to produce meaningful results.

Chapter 2

The Mysterious Success Factor

Before starting any board meeting, performing a 'puja' (prayer) was the first task for the owners of large industrial groups in India not many decades ago. Dressed in the traditional attire of a 'kurta' (an Indian collarless shirt) and a long coat with a turban or a round Indian cap, the owner would light an incense stick, a lamp and garland the deity, most likely the Goddess Lakshmi, the goddess of wealth and in many cases, the Supreme Lord Krishna. Then, a garland would be placed on the portrait of the late founder of the business or industrial group before getting down to taking management decisions with selected key managers. These family-owned enterprises are still some of the biggest in India and have become global players today, such asthe Birlas and the Singhanias. This tradition has survived for most shopkeepers and traders even to this day.

The modern management system offers no such prayers to the almighty before starting any board meetings. It is all very impersonal and profit - oriented. No wonder their decisions are not "*sattvic*" or oriented towards goodness and godliness. The total effort is to maximise profits—sometimes at any cost and by all fair and even unfair means. Their decisions are furtive to enable them to enjoy or produce enjoyment. But furtive activity is condemnable. The only way to extricate a person from his addiction to furtive work, as Krishna recommends, is *nishkama karma yoga*. The Supreme Lord emphasizes this important principle in the *Bhagavad Gita*:

Karmany evadhikaras te ma phalesu kadacana
Ma karma-phal-hetur bhur ma te sango 'stv akarmani
(Gita 2-47)

You have a right to perform your prescribed duty, but you are not entitled to the fruits of action. Never consider yourself the cause of the results of your activities, and never be attached to not doing your duty.

Most gurus explain only the first line. But they do not bother to explain the next line. If you possess an MBA in marketing, you have a right to become a Marketing Manager in some organization, but don't ask for any salary. Nobody follows this path because nobody is interested in spirituality. While attending a spiritual lecture by a guru addressing a crowd of 10,000 people, you will find many people discussing something else amongst them. Many people don't listen to the speaker. So anticipating a possible retort from Arjuna, the Supreme Lord Krishna says in the second line, "*Ma karma phala hetur bhur ma te sango'stv akarmani*." (The intention to enjoy the result of your activity should not be the cause of performing your action.) *Karma phal*—the result should not be the reason for your action. You may well ask, "If I am deprived of the results of my action, then what is the impetus for me to perform the action?" Krishna says, "Although there is no impetus, do not desist from performing any action." He says the results have to be given to Me. Satisfaction of the Supreme Lord Krishna is the impetus. This is the objective of a *Karma Yogi*.

But an executive cannot survive if he refuses the salary. If that executive is a Krishna Conscious person, he is basically a sinless person. He takes his salary just to make his livelihood. He spends his money and keeps something for the future and the rest he uses in spreading Krishna Consciousness. Right from the beginning, whether it is an individual or a corporate body, if the Supreme Lord Krishna or God is the centre of all activities, everything will go smoothly. An illustrious example was the great devotee of the Supreme Lord Krishna, His Divine Grace AC Bhakti Vedanta Shrila Prabhupada, the founding Acharya of the International Society for Krishna Consciousness (ISKCON) who practically lived a Krishna Conscious life. Before devoting himself full time to spreading the message of the Supreme Lord Krishna, he had a family and managed a pharmaceutical business.

The *Mahabharata* contains another example. Yudishthira, Arjuna and Bhima were all warriors engaged in war. They were trained in warfare and building their strength. But they were all devotees of the Supreme Lord Krishna. They were all successful. Duryodhana, who was as skilful as Bhima, and other great generals, failed because they relied on their own strength.

Two Extreme Options

You either have to accept God or Krishna Consciousness, lead a decent life based on morality as outlined in the *Gita* and follow a spiritual path, or you lead a Godless, fast life—earn money, enjoy physical pleasures, indulge in sinful activities, do not bother to walk on the spiritual path and die like an animal. These are the only two extreme options. So, to discourage the enjoyment of physical pleasures from *kamya karma*, one has to move towards *nishkama karma* and to offer the results of one's efforts to God.

Therefore, the principle of *Karma arpanam* is offering one's results to the Supreme Lord Krishna. This is required in our lives. Arjuna fought the war with full enthusiasm because he was committed to offer the results to the Supreme Lord Krishna. Hence, there was no let-up in his enthusiasm because he was not going to enjoy the results himself. Hence, he did not turn a fatalist and became victorious.

In the modern context of corporate culture, it is possible that if the CEO is Krishna Conscious that he will manage his company on ethical principles and that consciousness will percolate down the hierarchy. In my personal experience of the corporate world, the MD of an organization was scared of a sales person who was very honest. This was because the MD was a very dishonest person. So if the head is honest, others will automatically be very careful with him, at least in their dealings with him.

This is happening more and more these days. Since most business people are only interested in making maximum money, they usually overlook unethical practices. These could be in the form of short supplies of goods, lesser quantities of goods as compared to what is actually supplied, or making false expense claims, among many other things. At the corporate level, it can be bribing the officials to secure a contract or misrepresenting what is to be supplied. In this rat race, a single honest person is enough to upset the corrupt system.

They will understand that this person is above reproach and cannot be bought at any cost. People will stop all under-the-table dealings with him. Initially, they may not like him but then later, after working with a Vaishnava or Krishna Consciousness person or devotee, one will gradually start enjoying one's association with him and gradually give up all sinful actions. But this will not happen overnight.

All corporate activities in line with Krishna Consciousness cannot result in losses. On the contrary, profits can be guaranteed. Maharajah Ambarisha was the Emperor of the entire planet earth. It is said in the scriptures that he only used his legs to visit Vishnu temples, he only used his eyes to see Krishna's deities, his tongue was used only to taste Krishna *prasadam*, his ears only used to listen to the glories of the Supreme Lord. In this way, he had dedicated his whole body towards Krishna Consciousness activities. Then the question arises in our minds: how was he ruling the whole world? But he was and it was beautiful during his leadership. The Supreme Lord Krishna took care of it. He organizes everything properly for you once you have fully surrendered to Him.

It is only when you are genuinely into Krishna Consciousness that these things start happening. If you are not genuinely devoted to Krishna Consciousness, you have to face the situation that you are facing today. You cannot reject the Supreme Lord Krishna and try to implement the principles of the *Gita*. It is not possible. In the *Ramayana*, Ravana's policy was to reject Rama and try to enjoy Sita, the mother of the universe. Ravana was totally ruined. By rejecting God, or Krishna, the whole world is gradually sliding towards ruin. This is clearly seen as we are destroying the environment and ecosystems, propagating unfair financial systems, and supporting corrupt and oppressive governments in many countries of the world today. And most of all, the majority of the world's people is living in poverty when there are enough resources for everyone on this planet to have a reasonable standard of living.

The Final Resort

You may ask: what if a company goes bankrupt by following God or Krishna Consciousness? But it cannot. If you cannot accept this answer it is not your fault. This is because basically we do not have the faith that the Supreme Lord Krishna can do this for us. If you have the faith, you will see your company, your industry, the whole country—indeed the world—flourishing. No wonder, it is said, that faith can move mountains.

During Yudishthira's era, the earth used to produce all vegetables and grains without the soil being tilled. Automatically, they sprouted out. It is a problem now because we do not have faith in the Lord. It is not merely faith; we should rely a hundred per cent on the Supreme Lord Krishna.

There is a famous anecdote in the *Mahabharata* to prove this point.

Duryodhana invited the five Pandavas accompanied by their wife, Draupadi, to visit him in his new palace and throw the dice with him. The eldest Pandava, Yudishthira, played with him, and during these dice sessions, he lost everything: his kingdom, even himself and his brothers. Duryodhana was assisted by his uncle and a crafty cheat Shakuni. Finally, Yudhishtra was provoked in a 'winner takes all' game to stake his wife. He lost.

Now Duryodhana took his full revenge by ordering his brother Dushasana to bring Draupadi to the fully assembled court. When she declined, he dragged her by her hair into the main hall of the court packed with all royal elders and relatives, nobles and commanders, presided over by the blind king Dhritarashtra and his blindfolded wife, Gandhari. Then Duryodhana ordered Dushashana to strip her of her robe. Draupadi was sure that with so many brave and wise men and her close relatives, someone would save her. She screamed at her five husbands to save her. With his intellect, Yudishthira could have asked the men to let her go, the mighty Bhima could have crushed anyone who came near his wife, the brave warrior Arjuna could have killed anyone in combat. But, as slaves of Duryodhana, they fumed and flexed their muscles and remained motionless, silent and helpless.

All this time, the Supreme Lord Krishna and Rukmini were watching this scene on their monitor. Rukmini was persuading the Supreme Lord Krishna to go and help her. But the Supreme Lord Krishna replied, "No, she is depending on so many people. She is not calling Me. If she seeks My help, I will certainly respond." Rukmini said, "You are very cruel." Krishna said, "Well, this is the way I am."

Draupadi pleaded to the old and wise sages, the clan guru Kripacharya (guru of Dushasana) and the senior-most elder of the dynasty Bhishma Pitamaha, but the sages gave learned arguments for their inaction. The king and her father-in-law Dhritarashtra, the mother-in-law Gandhari, who heard her screams and frantic appeals, could have reprimanded their sons and stopped them from disrobing her. But they made feeble excuses to stop this despicable act. No one saved her. Ultimately, when she realized that everyone had let her down, she prayed to the Supreme Lord Krishna.

At this point, holding her sari with one hand, a desperate Draupadi cried, "Krishna!" The Supreme Lord Krishna's wife, Queen Rukmini said, "Now that she is calling You, please go and help her." He said, "No, she still has faith in her hand's ability but not full faith in Me." Queen Rukmini got angry and said, "You go away; I will help her." The Supreme Lord Krishna said, "Fine, go and help her." But Queen Rukmini was not even able to get up from her seat because she too was in the Supreme Lord Krishna's power. She could not move without the approval of the Supreme Lord Krishna. There is a famous saying that not a blade of grass can move without the Supreme Lord Krishna's approval.

Draupadi threw up both her hands in despair and beseeched the Supreme Lord Krishna for help. Queen Rukmini said, "Now look!".

"Now you see, she is totally relying on Me. I will go," said Lord Krishna. As the disgusting act of stripping Draupadi's sari was going on, by the all-pervasive presence of the Supreme Lord as paramatma even in each and every thread of the texture, the sari continued to extend yard by yard and would not end until Dushashana was exhausted and collapsed. Who had protected her? The Supreme Lord Krishna.

We have our ego and hence we think that our ability alone produces results in all our endeavours. This is not so. In Draupadi's case, it was a question of total faith. Only when she came to the point of relying a hundred per cent on the Supreme Lord Krishna did He help her. If you have that complete faith and surrender to Krishna, only then will He help you. He says in the *Gita*:

Ye yatha mam prapadyanrte tams tathaiva bhajamy aham
Mama vartmanuvartante manusyah partha sarvasah (4:11)

As one surrenders unto Me, proportionately I reward them.

So surrender is the key. The full hundred per cent. At first, it seems that by surrendering you become ego-less and you are trampled upon. But nobody can trample upon you. When you surrender totally, you become almost as powerful as God, by his kind empowerment. By Lord Krishna's mercy, Arjuna, and by Lord Rama's mercy, Hanuman, and by Lord Narasimha's mercy, Prahlada became invincible. Nobody could trample upon them.

A Merciless World

However, the corporate world is a merciless world. Executives and employees both act ruthlessly. They have no norms. Everything is calculated on profit and loss basis. Decisions are taken on the basis of results, productivity, breaking even when not profitable, optimum inputs, maximizing assets and minimizing liabilities. Forgetting about employee welfare, 'hire and fire' is the norm. Employees are not considered colleagues, but competitors. No wonder we have such unethical practices in the private sector with high prices, shoddy goods and services and workers' unrest and strikes.

When the Supreme Lord Krishna is with you, nobody can harm even one strand of your hair. How much faith and trust you have on Him is very important. When you accept the Supreme Lord Krishna a hundred per cent, He acts through you. So all your decisions and actions are '*sattvic*'.

What was Arjuna otherwise? What was his capacity? You know Bhishma Pitamah? He had defeated his own Guru Parashurama. You know Dronacharya? He was the teacher of all these students. How did Arjuna defeat all these people? Because the Supreme Lord Krishna was with him. When Krishna is with you, nobody can defeat you. Victory may sometimes be delayed as the evil may win at first but ultimately truth triumphs.

Thus Krishna Consciousness can be termed as the mysterious X Factor or the intuition claimed as the secret behind success by many executives. During my work as a marketing executive, I interacted with highly educated colleagues and asked them, "Do you believe in God?" Their answer was, "Well, I believe in some superpower." Actually, they were being arrogant. What is this superpower? He is all powerful. He is a person and not merely a power. He is energetic, and not merely energy.

An average person thinks that some power is helping him. No, it is actually a person. That intuition actually comes from *Paramatma*. The Supreme Lord Krishna's localized '*avatara*' or incarnation called *Vishnu* with four arms. Vishnu is residing in the heart of all living entities, even in small insects, ants, rats, elephants, plants and so on. It is this Vishnu who provides him with guidance at first. If the individual soul accepts it, he is successful; and if the individual soul does not want to acknowledge it, then He gives permission to that individual to act sinfully. So, it is the advice coming from the super soul, the Paramatma, which you think is your intuition.

But is this intuition helping a person to take negative actions? The Supreme Lord Krishna answers this question in the *Gita*:

> *Sarvasya caham hrdi sannivisto mattah smrtir jnanam apohanam ca*
> *Vedais ca sarvair aham eva vedyo Vedanta-krd veda-vid eva caham (15:15)*

I supply memory, power, knowledge and forgetfulness.

In the thirteenth chapter of the *Bhagavad Gita*, Krishna says He is *anumanta* which means that He gives the permission or sanctions. So, first He gives you the right ideas. If you reject them and you desire to act sinfully, then He gives you the permission to act sinfully. So, whether to act sinfully or righteously, sanction and empowerment is required from The Supreme Lord Krishna, and only then one can do it. That's why there is no place for ego here. You have to be ego-less.

What exactly is ego? Ego means you can act independently. Krishna says, "No. He is *Bharta*—the maintainer, *Bhokta*—the real enjoyer and *anumanta*, the approver. Krishna says, "So if you want to remember Me, if you want to acknowledge Me, pray for Me, I will give you power to do that. If you want to go against Me, oppose My views, execute your own ideas, your plans, your will, I will give you permission for the same. You will go your sinful ways."

In either case, the Supreme Lord Krishna empowers you, He gives you permission. You have no way to act independently. So where is the scope for arrogance? Your independence allows you only in desiring to obey or disobey Him. Initiating the desire to act piously or impiously is your move. But to perform that action, He has to empower you because you have no power to act on your own. It is all His will. This is clearly said in the *Bhagavad Gita*. He is called *Hrishika*, the controller of senses. *Hrishika* means senses, *isha* means controller. So, the Supreme Lord Krishna is in charge of your senses, not you. Where is your independence then?

Core Message for the Corporate World

If the corporate body, as a whole, or any individual owner, wants to perform his duty beautifully and live peacefully with positive results and achievements, he has to become a sinless person first. Anyone who has controlled his five physical senses is a human being. One who cannot control these senses is an animal. If a bitch is walking on a road at night and a dog attacks and jumps on her, it is considered 'animal behaviour'. But the same thing is happening today in the so-called human society.

Sexual harassment in the corporate world is common. The bosses routinely tease, molest assault, harass, grope and even rape their female employees. With greater awareness and human rights awareness among women, all this is resisted strongly. There is no doubt that tough new laws in developing countries like India are a deterrent and yet these horrible practices continue. However, in some cases, women tolerate this harassment because they need the job to support their families or gain promotions. So in these cases, the bosses get away with their carnal sins that are serious crimes now.

A woman is walking at 10 pm on a deserted road and a man attacks her and/or rapes her. These incidents happen all over the world today. The most horrendous rape case happened in New Delhi at around 9 pm on 16 December 2012. A young woman and her male friend boarded a bus at night. The six men in the bus, including the driver, hit the male friend until he became unconscious and then started to rape the woman in turns in the moving bus. After this horrific act, they threw out the woman and her male friend from the moving bus. The woman was admitted to a hospital and later flown to Singapore for treatment but she died. This case made young Indians livid with rage as huge public protests against the government for not providing adequate security and justice for women were held for many days in Delhi. Thousands clashed with the police. Similar protests took place in most major Indian cities and made national and international news for many days. The government hurriedly appointed a commission to look into this situation and propose legal reforms. This resulted in passing tough laws for sexual advances, harassment and rape.

A similar case happened on 22 August 2013 in Mumbai when a young photo-journalist was gangraped by five men in a deserted textile mill where she had gone on an assignment with her male colleague. The four accused tied the male colleague, raped the woman in turns and made a porn clip of their activity. The same gang carried out a similar rape on another woman on 31 July, which was later reported. The rapists were convicted. In Mumbai, a reputed businessman's son is alleged to have raped a woman the age of his mother. But more cases of rape continue with impunity.

What is the cause of these sex crimes? Almost all rapists are semi-educated young men exposed to 24-hour TV, movies, media and other negative influences that promote sex. The sexual energy of the young men is at the peak without any outlet. So they resort to this extreme action. If they were guided to the spiritual path at an early age and started loving the Supreme Lord Krishna by chanting the "Hare Krishna, Hare Krishna, Hare Rama Hare Rama, Rama Rama Krishna Krishna," their energies, including sexual energy, would be channelled for devotion and not desecration. In the corporate offices, if the executives follow Krishna Consciousness, they would not molest or rape their women employees.

Where is the difference between an animal and a man? Why can a dog not control its senses? Because it is an animal. But a man can control his senses, if he wants. So, if you can control your senses, you are human and if you cannot control them, you are an animal. And the answer is Krishna Consciousness.

The corporate world is flourishing with turnovers in billions—indeed trillions—of dollars. What is the use of these mammoth turnovers? Who are they benefiting? The rich are getting richer and the poor poorer. Inequality, crime, hatred, corruption are all increasing manifold. Humans are reduced to the level of animals. And you call it progress. And towards what end? If that is your aim, what is the use of thinking over implementing the principles of the *Gita* in corporate affairs? Godless advancement is advancement in ignorance. It is like a blind man advancing dangerously towards the end of a cliff top. This progress is just like sailing a fast but rudderless yacht.

Accept the existence of God—the Supreme Lord Krishna. Acknowledge His supremacy. Perform your activities like Arjuna did—only for His satisfaction. If you are the CEO, then you are the top leader of your organization and all its employees. Look after them. Ensure all of them become free from four major sinful actions. Spend at least half of your profits in creating spiritual awareness and propagating Krishna Consciousness.

Chapter 3

Ideal Chief Executive

While leading his commanders and their armies in the crucial war of Kurukshetra, the Supreme Lord Krishna knows that the odds are stacked against him—just like any CEO or Managing Director of a modern corporation. Basically, this situation is no different from a medium-sized, ethical company facing an unethical, huge, multi-national corporation that destroys competitors, breaks laws and bribes people.

The CEO for this dastardly Kaurava enterprise, Duryodhana, is consumed by greed for the Pandavas kingdom, just like a corrupt CEO feels when he plans to take over a competitor. He has more army divisions to fight his battle: eleven compared to seven for the Pandavas—just like many global corporations with far more funds, hell-bent to crush smaller companies. He has acquired the pitch of the conflict by using unfair means like trying to burn the Pandavas in a house made of lacquer, defeating them in a crooked dice game and then attempting to strip their wife in court. Many modern multi-national corporations sponsor gambling and strip shows with trips to Las Vegas for their clients and executives. Duryodhana is consistent in his evil pursuit by fair or foul means and not even the Supreme Lord Krishna can apparently convince him to abandon his evil intentions.

Leading the weaker side, the Supreme Lord Krishna realizes that the stronger evil might win. This is when enlightened corporate leadership and good management are critical for the company to survive and to thrive. When organizations are well managed, they can operate effectively and efficiently. Their chief executives must have very practical and clear plans. They must have organized structures, systems, and they must also evaluate results. When organizations are well led, they adapt to changes in the environment and develop cultures that inspire commitment and innovation. Both good management and enlightened corporate leadership are necessary to sustain organizational performance. Enlightened corporate leadership is possible only with Krishna Consciousness.

This means that the Chief Executive has to use every quality that is the hallmark of a great leader. Foremost among them is integrity. But this does not happen in the world today as the chief executives heading major corporations have their faults and drawbacks. Their mismanagement has led to the bankruptcy of some of the biggest corporations in the United States and all over the world. In the US, some major bankruptcies in 2008 have gobbled the savings of thousands upon thousands of shareholders and made thousands upon thousands jobless and homeless. At one time, these corporations were very respected market leaders but now they have filed for bankruptcy: Enron, General Motors, Chrysler, Lehman Brothers and many more. More than one hundred banks failed in the United States in the first nine months of 2009.

On July 11, 2008, the FDIC seized the assets of the largest Savings and Loan in Los Angeles and the 7th largest loan originator in the country. The seizure sparked rumors of bank runs. It also gave the public the first real Main Street glimpse of the Financial Crisis of

2008. IndyMac was founded in 1995 as Countrywide Mortgage Investment. Its purpose was to provide a means of collateralizing loans too high in value for Fannie Mae and Freddie Mac to service. At the time of its seizure, IndyMac held nearly $30 billion in assets, making it the fourth largest bank failure in history.

WaMu was America's largest Savings and Loan association, the sixth largest bank in the US and the largest bank failure in history. After a 10-day run on the bank in late September 2008, with total withdrawals in excess of $16 billion USD—almost 10% of the deposits—the FDIC seized WaMu's assets. JPMorgan Chase bought WaMu subsidiaries the next day for what many suspect at pennies on the dollar.

In Britain, Woolworths, an institution more than a retail chain store, closed down just before celebrating its hundredth anniversary. Other major British companies that went bankrupt included Barratts Shoes, Empire Direct, Nortel, Viyella, Waterford/Wedgewood, Motor World, Rosebys, to name a few.

In India, the CEO of a leading software company, Satyam, committed one of the biggest corporate frauds in modern times that went round the world as it had clients in many countries. The Satyam CEO, B. Ramalinga Raju, had created a world-class corporation and enjoyed all pleasures and honours of a top corporate leader. Success, money, fame and power...it was never enough for him, like the investment bankers of Wall Street. His Indian mindset prompted him to establish two major corporations in infrastructure and real estate for his two sons. To boost their chances of garnering contracts, he transferred huge amounts from Satyam to these companies. Just at this time, the real estate values plummeted, compounded with a liquidity crisis. In a last-ditch attempt, Raju tried to pay back Satyam funds by merging them with his sons' companies with disastrous results.

Would Krishna Consciousness have saved him from this mammoth disaster? Certainly, if he was working in the spirit of handling the Supreme Lord Krishna's money; if he had not resorted to stealing his company's assets; and if he had dedicated all his efforts, results and profits to the Supreme Lord.

Handling the Supreme Lord Krishna's Money

As the leader of any commercial organization, the Chief Executive or the MD should always remember that he is handling the Supreme Lord Krishna's property on behalf of Lord Krishna himself. So the results must be offered to Lord Krishna (*karma arpanam*). This automatically means that there is no room for any unethical business practices like bribery and corruption nor engaging in any illegal practices. These norms are brushed aside when the other directors demand high profits and/or the powerful competitors use these means to acquire greater market share. Basically, all these unfair and unethical business practices are the result of greed—for profits and personal gain. The Supreme Lord Krishna says:

> *There are three gates leading to hell—lust, anger and greed. Every sane man should give these up, for they lead to the degradation of the soul.*
>
> *Gita, Ch 16 – 21*

Thus, greed degrades the mind to devise these evil plans to degrade their souls as is evident from the actions of these CEOs.

Integrity and Leadership

Thus integrity, the integration of outward actions and inner values, is perhaps the foremost quality of corporate leadership. Such a

CEO can be trusted because he/she never veers from inner values, even when it might be expedient to do so; no matter what the circumstances. Leaders who consistently do the right thing will move steadily upward and onward. Integrity also means leading by example in all areas for all employees, consultants, customers or clients. It also includes keeping promises and abiding by all agreements without trying to wriggle out of them. And the Supreme Lord Krishna is the best role model in this respect.

Before motivating Arjuna to stand up and fight the battle of Kurukshetra, the Supreme Lord enlightened him with spiritual knowledge of the real self, the spirit soul so that he would become detached from identification with the physical body. Krishna said:

> *As the embodied soul continuously passes, in this body, from boyhood to youth to old age, the soul similarly passes into another body at death. A sober person is not bewildered by such a change. (Gita 2/13)*
>
> *For one who has taken his birth, death is certain, and for one who is dead, birth is certain. Therefore, in the unavoidable discharge of your duty you should not lament. (2/27)*
>
> *All created beings are unmanifest in their beginning, manifest in their interim state, and unmanifest again when they are annihilated. So what need is there for lamentation? (2/28)*

He reasoned with Arjuna that he might merely kill only the bodies of his relatives who were his opponents arrayed on the other side of the battlefield, and not the real persons—the spirit souls—residing in them. Giving up the body at the time of death is merely an act just like that of a person discarding a useless and worn-out set of jeans and a T-shirt and nothing else. This is because the conscious living entity, the spirit soul, neither takes birth nor dies.

After this enlightening discourse on the reality of spiritual existence, thus providing Arjuna with a spiritual framework from which to resolve his current predicament, the Supreme Lord Krishna doubts his capacity to instantly understand and assimilate spiritual knowledge. So He attempts to justify his participation in war even from the physical concept of life:

> *You have a right to perform your prescribed duty, but you are not entitled to the fruits of action. Never consider yourself to be the cause of the results of your activities, and never be attached to not doing your duty. (2/47)*

> *By being steadfast in yoga, O Arjuna, perform your duty and abandon all attachment of success or failure. Such evenness of mind is called yoga. (2/48)*

Finally, to galvanize Arjuna into action, the Supreme Lord Krishna says:

> *Therefore, O Arjuna, surrendering all your works unto Me, with mind intent on Me, and without desire for gain and free from egoism and lethargy, fight. (3/30)*

Thus the Supreme Lord Krishna displayed the true qualities of a brilliant leader by first preparing him for his message, delivering his message powerfully and motivating him to act.

Vision and Planning

The CEO must have a clear vision as to where he/she is steering the corporation. The aims should be well-defined and effectively communicated to everyone in the corporation. A good business leader knows where the company is going and has a precise plan on how to guide it in the right direction. The CEO should have a long-term policy and short-term aims to implement it; employ the core competencies of everyone; should be unique and practical. The Supreme Lord Krishna's vision meets all these criteria as it aimed at victory for the Pandavas and led them to achieve it.

Be it a tactful ploy or skilful strategy, perfect planning is a prerequisite for the successful execution when it comes to management. The Supreme Lord Krishna exhibited tremendous acumen in this regard. His aim was to rid the earth of the burden of demonic rulers, the evil kings of the Kaurava clan. To kill all of them, a great war was required. For this aim, His far-sighted planning began right from the time of His birth when he killed the wicked witch who came to feed him as a baby, after which he killed the evil king Kamsa.

Later, the Supreme Lord Krishna set the stage for the ultimate war when King Yudishthira's royal palace was constructed by Maya Danava with many wonderful and opulent features. When the envious Duryodhana entered the palace, bewildered by the craft of Maya Danava, he mistook parts of the solid floor for water and thus lifted his garment. In another spot, he fell into the water mistaking it for a solid floor. *Bhagavat Maha Purana* describes this scene:

> *My dear Pariksit, Bhima laughed to see this, and so did the women, kings and others. King Yudishthira tried to stop them, but the Supreme Lord Krishna showed His approval.* (10-75-38)

King Yudishthira tried to check the laughter by glancing at the women and Bhima. Lord Krishna, however, approved with a gesture of His eyebrows. Although Yudishthira tried to restrain Bhima and others, Lord Krishna lent His approval. The Lord knew that Duryodhana would definitely avenge his humiliation. This is significant for his long-term plan.

On another occasion, Krishna did not dissuade Yudishthira from gambling when invited by Duryodhana and Shakuni, knowing well the impending and disastrous consequences of the humiliation to be suffered by the Pandavas, and especially Draupadi. This deliberate connivance constitutes the core aspect of planning which positively culminated in declaring war among the cousins.

Once the Supreme Lord Krishna assisted Arjuna and his Pandava brothers living in disguise. During Draupadi's bridegroom-choosing ceremony *(swayamvara)*, the three Kaurava suitors—Duryodhana, Karna and Jarasandha—were deliberately insulted while the Pandavas married her. This antagonized the other assembled kings who later sided with Duryodhana in the battle of Kurukshetra.

The Supreme Lord Krishna abducted Queen Rukmini from a pre-marital ceremony and married her through the *Gandharva vivaha* process by exhibiting his chivalry. This infuriated kings like Shishupala and others assembled on the occasion against specific invitations from Rukmini's father, King Bhishmaka. This act pushed them to favour Duryodhana in the war at Kurukshetra.

These incidents graphically described in the most exalted classical epic *Mahabharata* demonstrate the far-sighted, effective and infallible planning of Lord Krishna that led to the great war of Kurukshetra.

Team Spirit

The corporate leader must be a team player because he/she requires the full support of all his staff. This means encouraging them, identifying their potential, motivating them, appreciating their efforts, listening to them with an open mind for their feedback, giving credit to them where it is due, and being fair to them at all times before passing his judgment or taking action. All this inspires them to achieve more. He should allocate assignments according to the nature—or the *dharma*—of his subordinates. Even as the captain, the Supreme Lord Krishna was a team player right from his childhood when he romped with His friends to steal butter until the great war at Kurukshetra and attained victory for righteousness when he inspired Arjuna to fight after convincing him that it was his *dharma*. When Arjuna was caught in a dilemma whether 'to fight or not to fight', the Lord chastised him as follows:

> *My dear Arjuna, how have these impurities come upon you? They are not at all befitting a man who knows the progressive values of life. They do not lead to higher planets, but to infamy.* (2/2)

> *O son of Prtha, do not yield to this degrading impotence. It does not become you. Give up such petty weakness of heart and arise, O chastiser of the enemy.* (2/3)

Compassion based on physical relationships was Arjuna's weakness that caused his reluctance to fight. The Supreme Lord Krishna exhorted him thus to overcome this misplaced compassion:

> *The bewildered spirit soul, under the influence of the three modes of material nature, thinks himself to be the door of activities, which are in actuality carried out by nature.* (3/27)

One who is in knowledge of the Absolute Truth, O mighty-armed, does not engage himself in the senses and sense gratification, knowing well the differences between work in devotion and work for positive results. (3/28)

Even a man of knowledge acts according to his own nature, for everyone follows his nature. What can repression accomplish? (3/33)

To boost his sagging morale the Lord exhorts Arjuna to do His bidding.

Therefore, O Arjuna, surrendering all your works unto Me, with mind intent on Me, and without desire for gain and free from egoism and lethargy, fight. (3/30)

The Lord wanted to impress upon Arjuna the urgency and the need to take a hard and bold decision and emphasize that the reluctance and diffidence to do so would only bring disaster. Sometimes the leader of a corporation is required to pull up an erring subordinate and be rough with him to bring the deviant back on track. Acting with this attitude the Supreme Lord initially chastised Arjuna with a strong rebuke. He reprimanded him for his display of impotent behaviour at the time of grave crisis, that is unbecoming of a true *kshatriya* warrior. 'Nobody can remain forever in this world. For one who has taken birth, death is certain and those who die are sure to take birth again,' the Lord concluded. Therefore, the Lord informed him that the real person is not killed when the physical body is slain.

In the course of this motivation, a leader invariably highlights the plus points or the positive aspects of a diffident subordinate as well as the prestige and recognition that he or she enjoys in the professional circle so as to re-ignite his or her spirit of performance. Thus, knowing Arjuna's fighting capacity as a renowned hero of his time admired and envied even by his enemies, the Supreme Lord impressed upon him that great generals like Bhishma, Drona, Kripa and Karna, who held him in high esteem, would now label him as a coward if he were to withdraw. Such a dishonour would be worse than death. He stressed this point to score the importance of his participation in the war since refusal would only tarnish his image and bring him into disrepute.

> *People will always speak of your infamy, and for one who has been honoured, dishonour is worse than death.* (2/34)

> *The great generals who have highly esteemed your name and fame will think that you have left the battlefield out of fear only, and thus they will consider you a coward.* (2/35)

> *Your enemies will describe you in many unkind words and scorn your ability. What could be more painful for you?* (2/36)

Earlier, Arjuna quoted the injunctions in *Dharma shastra* (religious scripture) saying that he would suffer sinful reactions if he were to kill his relatives in the battle. But the Supreme Lord addresses this concern directly by saying that He knows the actual import of all the *Vedas* and had compiled the *Vedanta* in His incarnation as Veda Vyasa. Armed with the most perfect knowledge, as a strong leader, the Supreme Lord offers perfect guidance to His friend and devotee Arjuna caught in a serious dilemma, by revealing to him the higher understanding of true scriptural purpose; thus repudiating his current faulty understanding. He says:

Considering pleasure and pain, gain and loss, victory and defeat to be equal, fight for the sake of fighting, you will never incur sin. (Gita 2/38)

Moreover, encouraging the confused warrior Arjuna, the Lord reveals the highest truth to him by highlighting the fact that Arjuna's engagement in the war was not merely a battle to be fought for gaining the kingdom but it is *bhakti* or devotional service to the Supreme Lord Himself. He says:

A person engaged in devotional service rids himself or herself of both good and bad karma even in this life. One who performs duty without attachment, surrendering results unto the Lord, remains unaffected by sinful action just as a lotus leaf is untouched by water. This is the real art of work.

Finally, eliminating all his doubts in one masterly stroke, the Lord reveals His universal form, as Arjuna sees that all great generals like Bhishma, Drona and Karna are being crushed between His teeth. Then, the Supreme Lord Krishna exhorts him:

Therefore get up. Prepare to fight and win glory. Conquer your enemies and enjoy a flourishing kingdom. They are already put to death by My arrangement, and you, O Savyasachi, can be but an instrument in the fight. (11/33)

Thus, the Supreme Lord Krishna systematically inspired, motivated and ultimately stirred Arjuna to act positively and perform his *dharma* or duty to fight evil.

Communication

All great leaders are great communicators for their employees, customers or clients; project partners and consultants in informing them of the corporate goals. They communicate clearly, articulately and regularly. The Supreme Lord Krishna displays the best qualities of a communicator as he explains the most intricate ideas in the *Gita* to his friend Arjuna and motivates him to fight when he is dejected and has laid down his bow and arrows.

Creativity and Courage

The ability to think differently and to see situations and potential that others have not seen is what constitutes creativity in corporate leadership. Above all, the CEO must have the courage to take risks as every enterprise has risks and unknown factors. Creativity and courage result in new initiatives, products, projects and markets. The Supreme Lord Krishna amply demonstrated all these qualities throughout His presence on this earth.

Organizational Ability and Tactics

To defeat great generals like Karna, Bhishma and Drona was a tough task. The Supreme Lord Krishna taught the Pandavas some effective tactics in that regard. During the fight with Karna, the Lord urged Arjuna to shoot him when he was trying to pull out the sunken wheel of his chariot from the mud—not according to the principles of war. During his battle with Bhishma, he asked Arjuna to keep Shikhandi, a eunuch, in front of him facing Bhishma. Seeing a eunuch, the true warrior Bhishma would lay down his arms. Arjuna took advantage of this advice and thus defeated the great general.

Similarly, Drona was defeated due to his attachment towards his only son Ashvattama. According to the Supreme Lord Krishna's advice, when false information of Ashvattama's death was announced, Drona fell prey and became heartbroken. Drishtadyumna took advantage of this situation and killed Drona.

In another instance, Arjuna took a vow of self-immolation should he fail to kill Jayadratha before sunset. All of Arjuna's endeavours failed and the sun was about to set. At once, Duryodhana brought Jayadratha in front of Arjuna and demanded fulfilment of his vow. Immediately, the Supreme Lord Krishna ordered Arjuna to kill Jayadratha and he did so because the sun had not actually set. It was merely covered by the Supreme Lord Krishna's *sudarshana*. Lord Krishna is eternally liberated and hence is beyond good and evil so He did not hesitate to use evil to defeat evil.

Personnel Management

In any industrial-cum-commercial enterprise, personnel management demands ingenuity. This is because, in management parlance, out of the four M's—

Men, Machine, Materials and Money, the M representing Men (which also includes women) is considered very crucial. In other words, without this M, that is personnel, the other M's become useless. In any organization, it is the intelligent staff with loyalty, intellectual integrity and financial honesty that forms its artery that accounts for its image, accelerated growth and attainment of goals.

In a sensitive exercise like the preparation for war, the Supreme Lord Krishna employed amazing skills in managing human resources. Since they were cousins, both Arjuna and Duryodhana called on the Supreme Lord Krishna to get His support in the forthcoming war. The Lord then offered to them to choose between

Himself and His Yadava army. However, Lord Krishna situated in the heart of every living being as *Paramatma* or the supersoul, inspired Duryodhana from within his heart to opt for the Yadava army. As a result, Arjuna was happy to have the Lord on his side. The Lord also ensured Arjuna the support of Shikhandi and Dhrishtadymna, the two arch rivals of powerful generals Bhishma and Drona, respectively, who played important roles in the ultimate victory. The Supreme Lord Krishna also indirectly involved Lord Parashurama whose curse was the main reason for Karna's death. The Lord also gave responsible assignments to youthful leaders like Abhimanyu, Ghatotkacha and the young sons of the Pandavas.

Of course, the far more powerful five Pandava brothers were the backbone of the entire exercise. *Yudhi* means 'in the battle'; *sthira* means 'steady'. Thus, one who is never perturbed and retains his composure by remaining steady through all trying situations during a battle is called Yudishthira. Arjuna was known as *Parantapa* which means the tormentor of enemies. *Bhima* means terrible. It is said that when Bhima walked on the battle ground, the whole earth trembled. Hence, the Supreme Lord Krishna placed him right in the forefront of his army to terrify the enemy. All these are some examples of the optimum use of human resources for best results.

Monitoring and Directing

Just like top marketing executives sometimes step out of their air-conditioned offices to interact with their field sales officers in the market to keep themselves abreast of the situation, the Supreme Lord Krishna was personally present in the battlefield with Arjuna and other Pandava brothers all through the eighteen days of the war.

He was providing guidance from moment to moment and took instant decisions. To ensure that all His plans were perfectly executed to produce the desired results, the Lord took instant decisions which were pragmatic, although some of them were technically unethical as in the case of saving Satyaki from Bhurishrava in their combat. Of course, the Supreme Lord Krishna is always beyond the duality of being moral or immoral as He is transcendentally situated. Thus at this level, there is no duality like ethical or unethical.

Rock Steady and Dancing

Under great stress, every CEO must retain his balance; and in this aspect the Supreme Lord Krishna is always rock steady in the cyclone of the *Mahabharata's* events, especially the Kurukshetra war. The God Krishna is popularly known for playing flute and dancing. Although He can destroy the whole universe by simply raising His eyebrow from His spiritual abode, He comes down to earth for enacting pastimes 'Leela', only to delight His devotees. He celebrates life by dancing and playing on His flute – no matter what the crisis or emergency, what the results.

When the Supreme Lord danced 'Rasa Leela' with the devotees of Vrindavana, even the swarms of bees sang in accompaniment. The reverberation made such a loud musical sound that the heavenly beings watching from the sky became jubilant. Indeed, even the moon and the stars became astonished and thrilled.

However, this should not be compared to modern-day 'Pop' music and 'tap-dancing' by Playboys in clubs and pubs influenced by liquor drinking or drugging. This passionate behaviour will only aggravate sinful inclinations and not make anyone really happy. The hands of anyone doing charcoal business at some time or the other are bound to become stained. Similarly, anyone involved in any type of material activity is definite to become tensed up or depressed at one stage or the other.

To combat the pressure of everyday heavy workload and to remain balanced, men can always sing joyfully 'Hare Krishna' Mahamantra in different melodious tunes with the accompaniment of modern musical instruments. They can dance with raised hands in front of Radha Krishna deities in the Krishna conscious temples/centres.

This transcendental nature of singing and dancing alone can keep corporate executives cool and composed in all trying situations. This is the only real stress buster. This essential quality of a modern CEO is not taught in business college nor included in any management book. This, remaining unperturbed in all circumstances, ultimate quality results from surrendering to the Supreme Lord.

Is Krishna Consciousness the only way to achieve corporate aims?

That is so because the whole world has become sinful due to Godlessness. Since the CEO is not into Krishna Consciousness, he will resort to corrupt tactics. It is a vicious cycle. That is why the *Gita's* principles cannot be implemented in a corporate body selectively unless fundamental requirement for Krishna Consciousness is accepted from top level management downwards..

In earlier days, the King and his Brahmin ministers were sinless persons. The public might have been sinful. They were punished, rewarded or reprimanded according to their actions. So the PR officer should see the Supreme Lord Krishna everywhere, that is to achieve *sama darshana.* Then only does he start respecting everyone and does not exploit anyone. All heads of various departments or functions should be directed to Krishna Consciousness so that they can guide and govern the subordinates under them in an appropriate way that can help in the healthy growth of an organization.

Chapter 4

Ideal Heads of Departments

Looking around his senior executives, the Supreme Lord Krishna sees that all the five Pandavas are not without their shortcomings—just like any directors of a modern corporation. Yudishthira, the eldest Pandava, the wise one, was always following truth and righteousness. According to the rules governing Varana-Ashrama (socio-religious) system prevailing then, kshatriyas should not refuse when invited for a dual combat or gambling. In his excessive eagerness to strictly adhere to the principles, unable to refuse invitation from the opponents he gambled away his empire and even his wife. Many executives, professionals and businessmen have lost their fortunes in Las Vegas casinos and other gambling venues. The great warrior and strongman Bhima could not resist over-eating delicious food. The overweight executives today show the same clamour for good food. The third eldest, the brave Arjuna, due to misplaced compassion was hesitant to fight his powerful cousins who had cheated him of his empire. Many executives give up leading from the front in the face of unfair business practices by their stronger competitors. The fourth Pandav Nakula, and the youngest Sahdeva, being young ones, prefered lighter form of engagements compared to ghastly warfare.

Each one of the Pandavas had failings. The odds were stacked high against them. And yet they succeeded! Why? Only because they were totally surrendered to the Supreme Lord Krishna and performed their actions as *Nishkama karma:* selfless effort dedicated to Him. Let us examine how the heads of departments in a modern corporation should be led by the Supreme Lord Krishna.

Head of Production Department

The Head of Production department should have the basic understanding that the Supreme Lord Krishna is the actually greatest producer, and he should simply say, 'I am just representing you and making things available to the public so that they are satisfied because I see You in everyone and everything.'

The Head of Production Department should always be conscious that the Supreme Lord Krishna is the original producer of everything. Then he cannot possibly ignore the principles of Krishna Consciousness to produce sub-standard products and/or services at high prices. By exploitative use of natural resources without replenishing them, our environment has been severely damaged and depreciated and is now well on the road to speedy destruction. The negative results from all this are global warming, polluted rivers, seas, vanishing forests and disappearing wildlife and fauna.

> *Natural resources belong to the land or the agents, and those who use them for gratification are thieves punishable by the laws of nature. Gita Ch 3 -13*

Nature has enough supply for everyone's needs. Because of our unlimited greed, we have been exploiting the earth's natural resources. We have committed sins by destroying natural resources and because of these sinful activities, the whole world is suffering.

Global warming is the consequence of our unreasonable and godless activities. Now, the commercial sectors and greedy persons have woken up to this disaster but their greed continues to exploit nature.

Production should basically depend only on agriculture. You require a healthy life and for that you require agriculture. The mass production of unlimited industrial products is not essential. Man has lived without most industrial products of today for thousands of years until the Industrial Revolution that happened a mere 200 years ago. By producing a multiplicity of goods and creating more and more demands, industrialization has consumed far too many of our limited natural resources. Moreover, industrialization has not made a happier man but a dissatisfied man clamouring for more and more. Today, the distinction between essentials, comforts and luxuries has become blurred. What was once a luxury, like a car, has become a comfort today. So, the answer to happiness and inner peace is not acquiring more physical goods, comforts and luxuries but reducing our excessive demands and focusing on Krishna Consciousness.

The Supreme Lord Krishna is the original producer of the basic five elements. The Production Manager will automatically know if he is a God-conscious person. Even Einstein said that Krishna is the real creator. God is the real creator. Newton acknowledged the existence of God. He said that the universe is made by God. If the Production Manager understands that the original producer is the Supreme Lord Krishna and who has produced the whole universe and the five basic elements (earth, water, fire, ether and air), then he will be successful in his work and will also make spiritual advancement. In fact, he should think every day that he is producing on behalf of the Supreme Lord Krishna and he is nothing compared to Him. Only then does he become a religious person and a diligent manager.

The only aim of human life is to attain spiritual liberation. Ignoring this aim, people have produced so many goods like cars and computers. To make the best use of a bad bargain, and since we have these facilities, we should be using them to spread Krishna's message. Do we really require all these mobiles, computers or white goods? But they can be used in serving the Supreme Lord Krishna and spreading His message. If I go by bicycle, I can reach only few people. But if I go by car, I can cover a much greater area like a big city and reach hundreds of people in a day. A car is not important for my personal use. It should be made available for spreading Krishna's message. So these facilities must be properly used for service to Krishna Consciousness and not for sinful pursuits like going to casinos and night clubs.

The Head of Marketing Department

If the products to be marketed offer good value for money, the role of the Marketing Manager becomes easier and in line with Krishna Consciousness. With sub-standard products and/or high prices the company indulges in sinful activities against Krishna Consciousness. Since advertising is a part of marketing, it should not proclaim false attributes to products or services or exaggerate their quality. Marketing manager must conform to high moral standards both in their depiction as well as descriptions to mislead people with false promises. He must desist from false alluring attitude just for the sake of promotion and sales. Lord Krishna marketed his ideas effectively to persuade the Pandavas to act in a manner that resulted in victory in the great battle.

The Head of Distribution Department

Once the goods are produced, they must be distributed to the wholesalers, retailers and, through them, to the consumers. Thus this department usually has a warehouse to store them, maintain their inventories, and transport them. The distribution centre stores the product until needed by the retailer and supply the correct model, size and quantity, as a company may produce thousands of different goods. Any mismatch or delay can result in grave losses. Most products have a 'high season' when they are in greater demand, such as before the festive seasons of Christmas in the West or Diwali or other festivals and *pujas* in India. Fast-moving products have to be replenished quickly by informing the Production Department. All this requires high organizational skills and instant responses by maintaining and updating database with regard to 'feet forward' and 'feedback' through market intelligence. This is where Krishna Consciousness comes into play – if the head of this department is doing all this for the Supreme Lord Krishna, he will make the right decisions promptly and keep the supply chain working smoothly by ensuring impartial distribution network without fear or favour.

The Head of Accounts/Finance Department

The primary function of an accounting department is to track all revenue and expenditures, and pay taxes. This means maintaining an efficient accounting system that records all transactions and preparing a Balance Sheet at the end of the 'accounting year'. 'Finance' is an administrative function that includes Financial Reports on the effects of management decisions on the future Balance Sheets and advice for the senior executives and the Board of Directors. Thus Financial Planning and Investment are important functions for the success of the corporation.

Since honesty and integrity are paramount here, only a person well advanced in Krishna Consciousness should be in charge of this department. Many companies keep a secret set of accounts for the director/owners and another set for informing the shareholders or for paying lower income-tax. The accountant should not manipulate accounts, should pay the correct taxes to the government. He should not be corrupt in dealing with colleagues or the government. He should be cost-conscious, utility-oriented, should not be extravagant for the sake of vanity. If he understands that he is handling Krishna's money, the results will be positive. A cashier of a bank is always conscious that millions of Dollars he handles actually belong to the bank. Similarly all rich men including the head of the finance department must know that the wealth actually belongs to Krishna and they're mainly His cashiers.

Before providing examples of advanced accounting during the time of the Supreme Lord Krishna, it is important to note that many aspects of accounting in those ages were taken for granted. For example, the emperors collected taxes from thousands upon thousands of people and kept full records of these payments. The ministers in charge of these taxes maintained records of all taxes received and all amounts spent for public welfare. Managing huge armies by these kings and emperors also involved advanced accounting for their purchasing, inventories, distribution and replacements. The armies on the Kurukshetra battlefield consisted of millions of men and all of them had full records. According to new research, the Arthashastra of Kautilya mentions double entry bookkeeping for these records.

During Vedic times, finance was usually raised by performing a *yajna* sacrifice. To collect finance in the form of taxes, Lord Krishna permitted Yudishthira to perform *Rajasuya yajna* in response to His request. On getting the Lord's approval, King Yudishthira assigned zonal targets for each direction to his four brothers. He sent Sahadeva to the south, Nakula to the west, Arjuna to the north, and Bhima to the east.

After defeating many kings with their prowess, these heroic brothers brought back abundant wealth for Yudishthira

Maharaja, who was intent on performing the sacrifice, O King.
(Srimad Bhagavatam, Canto 10, Ch 72, Text 14)

By dispatching his younger brothers to collect taxes in four different directions, Emperor Yudishthira did not actually intend that they declare war on the kings but to inform the respective kings about his intention to perform the Rajasuya sacrifice. So the local kings were required to pay taxes for carrying out the sacrifice. This payment of taxes to Emperor Yudishthira meant that a king accepted his supremacy over him. If a king refused to pay up, there was a battle for sure. Thus, by their influence and strength, the brothers conquered all the kings in all directions, and brought in plentiful taxes and gifts for King Yudishthira. Since Arjuna's contribution was the highest, he came to be known as *Dhananjaya, the winner of wealth*. Thus, the wealth collected through the Rajasuya yajna was so abundant both in quantity and variety that even Indra, the king of heaven, felt inferior.

The Head of Human Resources Department

Human resource management is a skill that attracts and nurtures talent. Every company needs to attract the most qualified and suitable employees and this is the challenge of the head of the Human Resources Department to recruit, nurture, motivate and reward them. Thus he must be compassionate as well as strict when required to deal with defaulters.

To get optimum output from the staff, skilful human resource management is required. The selection of personnel for different jobs should be based on the basic nature of the personnel because everyone is born with some innate qualities. The Supreme Lord Krishna applied the same principle. When the Lord wanted to annihilate the evil King Duryodhana and his men, He sought the able assistance of Arjuna, famous for his archery. Arjuna had kshatriya blood. The Supreme Lord Krishna did not seek help from the Brahmin sage Narada who would have readily obliged him. Hence, a job should be assigned on the basis of the inherent nature of an employee. Overall, he must assign the right people for the right jobs in line with the concept of division of labour and their inherent qualities as outlined by the Lord himself.

According to the three modes of material nature and the work ascribed to them, the four divisions of human society were created by Me. And, although I am the creator of this set, you should know that I am yet the non-doer, being unchangeable.

(Bhagavat Gita, Ch 4, Text 13)

Brahmins, ksatriyas, vaisyas and sudras are distinguished by their qualities of work, O chastiser of the enemy, in accordance with the modes of nature.

Peacefulness, self-control, austerity, purity, tolerance, honesty, wisdom, knowledge, and religiousness–these are the qualities by which the Brahmins work.

Heroism, power, determination, resourcefulness, courage in battle, generosity, and leadership are the qualities of work for the ksatriyas.

Farming, cattle raising and business are the qualities of work for the vaisyas, and for the sudras there is labor and service to others.

(Bhagavat Gita, Ch 18, Texts 41, 42, 43 & 44)

Most major corporations have more departments due to the size of their operations.

The Head of Research and Development Department

All efforts should be directed to develop products for use that should not disturb the balance of nature—this means that they should be eco-friendly. If the Head of R&D is Krishna Conscious, he will automatically design and develop eco-friendly products. Much research has been carried out by Western countries to develop products that have resulted in global warming. We should always remember that the Supreme Lord Krishna is the ultimate creator and controller of nature.

The Head of Planning Department

Plans must first be submitted for approval to the Supreme Lord Krishna. Within the corporate body, as a Planning Head, he should be a cost-conscious person. He should plan intelligently and with proper budgeting. He should feel in his bones that he is handling Krishna's money. Setting goals means increasing the demand of the product, but the plan should first be approved by Krishna. The moment I get up in the morning, I fold my hands and say, '*Hey Krishna hridi sthitena tvaya yatha niyukto'smi tatha kromyaham*", "*O' Supreme Lord Krishna you are living in my heart. I will operate in the way you engage me*". The way you will engage me, I will operate.' Only then do I get up from my bed. If the Planning Manager has this understanding, the Supreme Lord Krishna will guide him fully in his plans.

In the *Gita* (15/15), Krishna says, *mattah smriti, janam, apohanamcha*; 'I supply memory power, intelligence and forgetfulness.'This means Krishna will give the Head of Planning the required intelligence. Some modern-day scientists admit that they suddenly stumble upon an idea when they are relaxed—what they do not know is that Krishna Consciousness has taken over! That idea is supplied by Krishna's partial representation situated in everyone's heart as four-handed paramatma or supersoul.

The Head of Public Relations (PR) Department

Projecting the correct image is the major priority of the PR department, but in the modern corporate sector, this is ignored many times. Many a time, a false image is created and presented. Or, an ugly truth is whitewashed by slick PR practices by bribing the media. All these are sinful activities. The head of PR should realize God's presence in everyone. So he should respect everyone. It is called as *Maanada*. He should build healthy relations on the basis that every living entity is Krishna's expansion. They deserve respect and reverence and so he should develop friendly and pleasant relationships. But many PR executives do not follow this in the corporate world. They resort to sycophancy to please the media or powerful or influential persons. He then can improve or project the right image of the company. If you have an idea that this person to be influenced is corrupt and by supplying him with a bottle of imported whisky, you can get anything done, then what image of the organization will you project? In this manner, the PR executives actually harm the image of the organization in the long run. But if the PR head is a truly Krishna Conscious person, he will not engage in such bribery to impress anyone. Only a devotee with good character and pleasant mannerism can project a proper image of an organization.

The Head of Technology and IT Department

Technology should ease and improve workers' operative effectiveness. Technical innovations must aim at reducing workers' physical input and mental stress to improve their efficiency. Technology that harms the natural environment must never be used. Similarly, Information Technology should ease the repetitive tasks of the desk workers and upgrade operating systems and procedures.

Greed and Corruption

Greed and power are the main reasons for corruption by corporates the world over. Increasing turnover by securing big contracts or orders is a major reason for corruption. The other reason is to get corporate power with a bigger share of the market and reduce cut-throat competition. India is one of the major emerging markets tied down by corruption and has made international news with some of the scandals and scams in the last few years involving billions of dollars. Corruption is ingrained in almost all developing countries but its scale and extent in India has corroded the country's image.

A survey on corruption in India by a leading accountancy and consulting firm, KPMG, showed that in 2011 61 per cent of the respondents believed that India will stay the same or get worse. In fact, by 2013, it did get worse. Major scandals and scams involving billions of dollars surfaced and this became a national concern before the general elections in 2014. The top three corrupt scams were Commonwealth Games construction contracts, 2G Spectrum and assigning coal mining contracts, among others. Real estate projects are marred by a high degree of unethical practices by the developers and their agents. This is due to a major amount of the price is in unaccounted cash. Major government projects for social welfare also provide a great scope for creaming off funds at every level by the politicians and the civil servants.

It is pertinent to examine here how every department of a company indulges in corruption based on greed. Here are a few instances of greed that translates into corruption and unethical means for the different departments of a company:

Production – Using low-quality raw materials, saving costs by damaging the environment or supplying less than the specified quantity.

Distribution – Billing more than the actual supply or supplying unauthorized dealers.

Marketing – Products or service do not conform to promises made.

Finance – Under or over-invoicing or hiding income to pay less tax.

Human Resources – Paying less than the legal wages or not paying due benefits.

Research and Development – Stealing new research from other companies or organisations or not paying royalties.

Planning – Stealing ideas and/or plans or poaching staff from competitive planning departments of competitors.

Public Relations – Releasing incorrect information, hiding the truth during crises or bribing the media to publish company news.

Technology and IT – Installing unsafe production machinery that injures workers or using illegal computer programs. The data generated must not be used for unethical purposes.

If a company is managed with the principles of Krishna Consciousness, any of these illegal and unethical practices would never be carried out. The CEO following the Supreme Lord Krishna would rather have reasonable profits than compromise by indulging in these corrupt practices.

During Vedic times, austere and sense-controlled beings whose minds were thoroughly purified communicated over long distances without the help of communication instruments. Similarly, such pure souls could empower others too. Hence, Sanjay, the Personal Assistant of Dhritarashtra, was gifted with special powers by the sage Veda Vyasa, the author of the *Mahabharata*. This enabled Sanjay to inform King Dhritarashtra in real time the happenings on the battlefield by sitting in their room as if watching a giant TV monitor and providing running commentary on the action very much like satellite TV today.

In *Bhagavata Mahapurana*, we find that a qualified Brahmin boy of about ten years of age Sringi cursed Emperor Parikshit to die within seven days after being bitten by a snake called Takshaka. The sound of this curse reached all the planetary systems of the universe. The snake Takshaka who was to carry out this instruction also heard it although he was living in the nether regions, patala, millions of miles below the earth at that time. Is this the same as satellite broadcasting?

To top it all, Lord Krishna informs Arjuna that he uses a unique method of communication:

> *I am seated in everyone's heart, and from Me come remembrance, knowledge and forgetfulness. By all the Vedas am I to be known; indeed I am the compiler of Vedanta, and I am the knower of the Vedas.*
>
> *(Bhagavat Gita, Ch 15, Text 15)*

The Supreme Lord is situated in everyone's heart, O Arjuna, and is directing the wanderings of all living entities, who are seated as on a machine, made of the material energy.

(Bhagavat Gita, Ch 18, Text 61)

Is Krishna Consciousness the only way for achieving corporate aims?

Of course. In fact, Krishna Consciousness should be the corporate culture. In the case of the five Pandavas, the result was victory when they followed—indeed, surrendered to—the Supreme Lord Krishna. Once the CEO surrenders to the will of the Krishna, all heads of all departments automatically follow suit and it filters down to all employees as the corporate culture. The results, invariably, will be positive.

Chapter 5

Modern Management Techniques

The logistics of managing a war room are no different from taking decisions in a boardroom. The Supreme Lord Krishna gets reports that after ten days of battle at Kurukshetra, the Pandavas are losing. He has to deploy His resources—men and materials—in a new assault. A daringly new strategy needs to be worked out. The strategy has to be communicated or marketed to his commanders and implemented urgently to turn the tide. An exact tally of millions of his men, weapons, war animals and supplies for full logistical support is required to move into action.

In a modern corporation, the CEO and his directors would consider these matters under modern labels such as Human Resources Management, Strategic Management, Operations Management, Financial Management, Marketing Management and Information Technology Management. These modern names cover the basic operations that were equally important thousands of years ago. Assigning and deploying personnel for various tasks is now termed as Human Resources Management, the entire process of production for goods and services comes under Operations

Management, what was termed 'planning' is now termed Strategic Management, while accounting and finance come under Financial Management, promotion and sales are taken care of with Marketing Management and, finally, the new element over the last three decades, managing computer systems is dubbed as Information Technology Management.

Human Resources

This new term is now used for 'Education' as in the Ministry of Human Resources in the Government of India and is also used for what is previously termed as personnel management in the corporate sector. In the latter context, it covers how people are managed by organizations. In this new 'avatar' it includes the link between individual talent and organizational success using Psychology and other concepts. The traditional use in corporations and businesses refers to the individuals within a firm or agency, and to the department dealing with recruiting, training, firing and other personnel issues.

Operations Management

The traditional 'Production Department' is now renamed as Operations Management. This department involves managing the process that converts inputs (in the forms of materials, labour and energy) into outputs (in the form of goods and services). The difference between the production of goods and services has become difficult as companies combine goods with services. Operations Management aims to increase the content of value-added activities in any given process.

Starting preparations for the coming war well ahead, the Supreme Lord Krishna promoted the Pandavas to amass powerful weapons when they were in exile and unaware of the armed conflict. They acquired various weapons like *Agneya astra* (fire weapon), *Varuneya astra* (water weapon), *Vayvastra* (tornado weapon) among others. Apart from these, various demigods like Indra, the king of heaven, also gifted valuable missiles to the Pandavas. Lord Shiva personally came in disguise and demanded a combat from Arjuna. In appreciation of Arjuna's valour, the Lord presented him with a deadly weapon known as *Pashupata astra*. Arjuna was also proficient in *Brahmastra*, more advanced than today's nuclear missile.

The Supreme Lord Krishna had the fire God *Agni* donate a chariot to Arjuna that had infallible mobility and manoeuvrability. The Lord also ensured invincible Hanumanji's services by his presence as the emblem on the flag of Arjuna's chariot which is a definite sign of victory. Dronacharya once had Arjuna defeat Drupada to settle his personal scores with him. Feeling the humiliation, Drupada begot a son by name Drishtadyumna from a fire sacrifice purely to take revenge against Dronacharya with a vow to kill him. Knowing this well, Lord Krishna secured the services of Drishtadyumna in the Kurukshetra battle, who organized military phalanxes.

Strategic or Institutional Management

The new name for Planning Department, Strategic or Institutional Management involves drafting, implementing and evaluating decisions that will enable an organization to achieve its long-term objectives. This is the process of identifying and creating an organization's mission, vision and aims; developing policies and plans to achieve these aims and then employing resources to implement them. Finally, it includes monitoring them and evaluating their performance. In brief, setting goals, employing tactics and overseeing it all.

The Supreme Lord Krishna had conceived his masterplan right from His birth. His primary objective was reducing the growing power of the demons and relieving people from their cruelties. The secondary objective was fighting the historical battle in Kurukshetra in order to deliver justice to the Pandavas. Starting with the killing of demons like Putana, sent by the evil king Kansa for Krishna's life, He went on killing many demons in his childhood. He tamed the serpent Kaliya who previously poisoned the waters of River Yamuna, thus causing death of many cowherds. Finally, the Lord killed Kansa and thus flawlessly executed His plans.

He outlined his objective very clearly in the *Gita*:

> *Wherever and whenever there is a decline in religious practice, O descendant of Bharata, and a predominant rise of irreligion—at that time I descend Myself.*
>
> *In order to deliver the pious and to annihilate the miscreants as well as to re-establish the principles of religion, I advent Myself millennium after millennium. (4/7 & 8)*

Formulating strategies is a vital function in any form of business. Proper implementation of corporate policies that yield the desired results basically and fully depend on correct strategies employed. It demands alacrity, profound sense of judgment and an ability to manipulate intelligently. Therefore, this crucial activity is handled by the top-management.

In case of Mahabharata war management, the Supreme Lord Krishna adopted the same principle. He took over the job personally. He was like the Chairman and the five trustworthy loyal Pandava brothers were like a board of directors. The Supreme Lord Krishna ensured that Drishtadyumna was the CEO, who arranged the military formation—because Drishtadyumna was begotten though a fire sacrifice with the specific objective of killing Drona who was otherwise absolutely indefatigable since he was the martial teacher of the princes of the entire Kuru dynasty. Lord Krishna acquired the services of Shikhandi, a eunuch, who had also undergone gender transformation from female to male (this person was originally the queen Amba whom Bhishma refused to marry when she offered herself voluntarily) through severe austerity solely with an aim to avenge Bhishma for this humiliation. The Supreme Lord Krishna was aware of this. Enlisting Drishtadyumna and Shikhandi on the side of the Pandavas was the most skilful and important strategy of the Supreme Lord Krishna without which the Pandavas could not have won the Kurukshetra war because both the powerful generals Bhishma and Drona were invincible.

The very selection of the battlefield Kurukshetra was an important strategy. According to Vedic literature, natural elements like water, air and land influence every activity in this world. The Supreme Lord Krishna knew this aspect very well 5,000 years ago that the land of Kurukshetra was the most pious place mentioned in ancient scriptures. Pious persons like Krishna's father Vasudeva had performed many sacrifices here. Since he resides in the heart of everyone, the Supreme Lord Krishna inspired both the Kauravas and the Pandavas to decide on Kurukshetra as the battlefield to settle their scores because He was sure that the venue would favorably influence the pious Pandavas to emerge victorious.

To evaluate cross-functional decisions taken in all the war segments and to oversee effective implementation of all strategies in all spheres of operations, the Supreme Lord Krishna agreed to act as the driver of Arjuna's chariot. This gave Him a vantage point from where to take instant decisions and issue full directions to all. In political diplomacy or a business deal, skilful negotiation is an important element. The Supreme Lord Krishna was very adroit in such transactions. He nevertheless adhered to, and had full knowledge of, the Vedic principles governing such affairs. Accordingly, the Supreme Lord applied the four techniques of negotiation which are: *sama* (conciliation or peaceful approach), *dana* (compromise or concession), *bheda* (creating dissension amidst the adversaries), and *danda* (punishment).

First of all, the Supreme Lord went as an emissary of the Pandavas to Duryodhana's camp and peacefully requested their share of the kingdom as they had fulfilled the conditions of exile imposed upon them. This is *sama* (peaceful approach). When Duryodhana's response was not encouraging, the Supreme Lord demanded at least the control of five villages because as Kshatriyas, the Pandavas should not earn their livelihood by any other means according to Vedic injunction. This is *dana* (compromise).

When this failed to evoke any favourable response, the Supreme Lord sowed the seed of dissension in the enemy camp by refusing the offer of a delicious lunch with Duryodhana on the pretext that he had no appetite. At the very same time, he stopped on the road in front of Vidura's home and requested for a meal when Duryodhana and others were observing from the backyard of their palace. The Supreme Lord also tried to woo Karna to the Pandavas' side by revealing to him the secret of his birth. In other words, the Lord informed Karrna that he was also *Kaunteya* (the son of Kunti) and not *Radheya* (son of a charioteer). But Karna did not oblige the Supreme Lord. This is *bheda* (creating dissension in the enemy camp). Finally, the Supreme Lord declared war. This is *danda* (imposing punishment). These techniques are very much seen in action today in corporate as well as political negotiations.

He aimed to totally finish all demonic rulers like Duryodhana, Jarashandha, Kamsa, Shishupala at the end of Dwarpara yuga. He appeared on this planet with determination to accomplish this objective and succeeded.

Marketing Management

Instead of the old-fashioned 'Sales Department' with a Sales Manager, the modern corporations have a Marketing Department with a Marketing Manager who implements Marketing Management techniques. Marketing Managers are often responsible for influencing the level, timing and composition of customer demand with promotion, advertising and Public Relations. Thus, the Marketing Manager with his budget, staff and network, turns into a General Manager for a product. So the scope of marketing management is very wide to cover any activity or resource the firm uses to acquire customers and manage the company's relationships.

Traditionally, marketing consists of four factors: Product, Place, Promotion and Price. Of these four Ps, promotion is very vital. An organization may manufacture a quality product of a very high standard, identify a very ideal market segment and offer the product at a very attractive price. Yet, the product may turn out to be a damp squib if not promoted intelligently through effective publicity. A marketing team becomes effective only if it can fetch the real value of the product it markets and not merely recover its cost according to the price structure formulated by the company's Cost Accountant. To achieve this, promotion of the product is crucial.

A promotional scheme is normally based on the demand, purchasing capacity, taste and psychology of target-consumers. It must hit the bull's eye to attract and tempt them and push them to the sales counter of the shopkeepers through whom they ultimately purchase the product without fail.

On reaching the battlefield of Kurukshetra, the Supreme Lord Krishna successfully marketed the idea to a reluctant Arjuna to get up and fight when he heard that the originally enthusiastic Arjuna now appeared disinclined to fight. Since this inaction would jeopardize the accomplishment of the Supreme Lord's objective of annihilating the demonic kings present on the scene, he persuaded Arjuna to stand up and fight with various insights. At the outset, the Supreme Lord imparted Arjuna with the actual identity of a living being as a spirit soul and not body.

For the soul there is never birth nor death. Nor, having once been, does he ever cease to be. He is unborn, eternal, ever-existing, undying and primeval. He is not slain when the body is slain.

O Partha, how can a person who knows that the soul is indestructible, unborn, eternal and immutable, kill anyone or cause anyone to kill?

As a person puts on new garments, giving up old ones, similarly, the soul accepts new material bodies, giving up the old and useless ones.

(Gita 2/20, 21 & 22)

Even going by the bodily concept of life, the Lord argued, Arjuna should not desist from fighting.

Considering your specific duty as a ksatriya, you should know that there is no better engagement for you than fighting on religious principles; and so there is no need for hesitation. (2/31)

O Partha, happy are the ksatriyas to whom such fighting opportunities come unsought, opening for them the doors of the heavenly planets. (2/33)

O son of Kunti, either you will be killed on the battlefield and attain the
heavenly planets, or you will conquer and enjoy the earthly kingdom. Therefore get up and fight with determination. (2/37)

With instant alacrity and an excellent grasp of situation that could ruin his aim, Lord Krishna cajoled Arjuna to fight not by sermonizing but by convincing him that it is the only and the right path. Lord Krishna drove home the very inevitability of Arjuna's engagement in the war with a killer instinct of a very mature and a seasoned marketing executive with an impressive track record. He said,

Under illusion you are now declining to act according to My direction, But, compelled by your own nature, you will act all the same, O son of Kunti. (18/60)

He emphatically said that Arjuna should not hesitate to follow the Lord's directions.

If you do not act according to My direction and do not fight, then you will be falsely directed. By your nature, you will have to be engaged in warfare. (18/59)

Thus Krishna explained in detail all the pros and cons to Arjuna and then waited for his reaction. Arjuna responded saying:

My dear Krishna, O infallible one, my illusion is now gone. I have regained my memory by Your mercy, and I am now firm and free from doubt and am prepared to act according to Your instructions. (18/73)

Financial Management

The previous title of 'Accounts Department' has given way to the Finance Department. Due to our complex, modern economy, more functions have to be managed in the Finance Department. These include banking, budgeting, spending, raising, saving, planning and investing funds. For a public-quoted company on the stock exchange, it involves more complex areas of operating under the Company Law. Thus, most big companies have a Financial Manager or Director.

For all these functions, the basic principles of Krishna Consciousness apply in the same manner. These include honesty, transparency and, above all, accountability to everyone—the employees, the shareholders, the directors and the government.

Information Technology Management

This expertise covers understanding and identifying Information Technology as a corporate resource for achieving its overall aims for efficiency, profits and customer satisfaction. Since most technology is computerized these days, IT has become an integral part of Operations Systems in addition to accounting, inventories, personnel, administration and information systems.

Computers handle massive amounts of data usually organized in databases. A *database* is a collection of data that is organized so that its contents can easily be accessed, managed, and updated. If one considers that the Pandavas had 3.2 million armed personnel and the Kauravas had over five million armed personnel making a total of 8.2 million, then one can appreciate the extent of data management required. The army officers and commanders were required to maintain full records about these men, and maintain massive inventories of their supplies, equipment and animals (horses and elephants). This would certainly require very advanced systems of data management, perhaps the same as modern computerized databases.

Before providing examples of advanced technical inventions during the time of the *Mahabharata*, it is important to note many lethal rockets and other weapons that released smoke, fire, wind and water were deployed during this battle. These are as modern as any rockets and nuclear missiles of today.

All great scientists and the inventors of all modern amenities must have been unsuccessful yogis in their past lives. Otherwise, how would one logically explain the astounding inventions of airplane, telephone, radio and other inventions, since the Wright Brothers, Alexander Graham-Bell and Marconi never studied in any technical institution. Aeronautic engineering, telecommunication engineering and radio engineering colleges came into existence only after their inventions. Thus, it can be assumed that these ancient scientists were equally adept at inventing and used these devices in some form.

That many ascetics and yogis had such mystic powers in ancient India is common knowledge. In this context, the 34th verse of the 16th chapter of 3rd canto of *Bhagavata Mahapurana* states:

> *The activities and characteristics of the ethereal element can be observed as accommodation for the room for the external and internal existences of all living entities, namely, the field of activities of the vital air, the senses and the mind.*

The mind, the senses and the vital force, or living entity, have forms, although they are not visible to the naked eye. Form rests in subtle existence in the sky, and internally it is perceived as the veins within the body and the circulation of vital air. Externally, there are invisible forms of sense objects. The production of the invisible sense objects is the external activity of the ethereal element, and the circulation of vital air and blood is its internal activity. That subtle forms exist in the ether has been proven by modern science by transmission of radio, television and satellite signals transmitting text, pictures and films round the globe today by the action of the ethereal element.

Creative Problem Solving

After sharing many valuable insights, the Supreme Lord Krishna finally wants Arjuna to understand that there are no material solutions to material problems because He says this very world we inhabit is full of miseries and is temporary, *dukkhlayam* and *ashashvatam*. The *Bhagavata Mahapurana* also supports the Lord's claim describing it as *Dukhaushadham tadapi dukkham*—a solution to a problem later on looms as a larger problem than the original one.

The Supreme Lord says the final solution lies only in attaining the spiritual planet where He resides. Otherwise, merely by performing various pious activities on this earth one cannot move out of the cycle of *karma* or solve the problem of repeated birth and death. This is because both pious and sinful activities are material and such actions will cause one to rotate within this mundane *karma* cycle and not provide liberation from this bondage. The Supreme Lord assures that once we gain residence in His spiritual planet, we do not come back to this world. Therefore, the ultimate solution is to go beyond bodily concept and recognize one's true identity as a spirit soul and one's eternal relationship with the Supreme Lord Krishna, the Supreme spirit soul.

A classic example is the invention of the motor car. Initially, people felt happy as a car helps us in covering long distances in a short time and saves us from carrying loads of goods from place to place. Every rich man thought it was a great boon as the car helped him to commute from home to office and to any other place. Now this solution to transport us has created greater problems for us. With millions of cars on the roads of all urban areas of the world, and many more millions being added every year, our towns and cities are choking with traffic and being brought to a standstill with traffic jams, bottlenecks, congestions, gridlocks and environmental pollution leading to stress for the drivers and even road rage that ends in violence and deaths. So, governments all over the world are forced to construct multi-lane highways, expressways, flyovers, multi-storied car-parks and other infrastructure to ease traffic. Commuters park their cars at the nearest metro train stations and go to their offices by train. Due to the practice of travelling by car, walking has been reduced to the minimum. Thus, people suffer from various diseases and disorders. Finally, the constant increase in fuel price also increases the blood pressure of car-owners compelling one to re-think whether one should continue keeping a car at all.

Therefore, the Supreme Lord Krishna compels Arjuna to think about the ultimate problem beyond the current problems at Kurukshetra. The ultimate problem is *janma mritu jara vyadhi dukha doshanu darshanam*, the perception of evil of birth, death, old age and disease (*Gita* 13/9). Now all the global space scientists are vying with one another to intensify their explorative skills to ascertain the possibility of human settlement on Mars. This may sound like an innovative response to the current crisis of increasing population but not a credible solution. Even if they succeed in their attempts in this case or in regard to any other planet, problems will remain. No matter on which planet we reside, according to the Vedic literature, birth, death, old age and disease will continue to plague living beings all over the universe.

The Supreme Lord Krishna addresses this problem squarely. The Lord affirms that freedom from material bondage and performing loving devotional service to Him at His transcendental abode is the only true and permanent solution to the problems on this planet. To achieve this, while operating within this material world, the Lord advises Arjuna to work on the following basis:

> *Work done as a sacrifice for Vishnu has to be performed, otherwise work causes bondage in this material world. Therefore, O son of Kunti, perform your prescribed duties for His satisfaction, and in that way you will always remain free from bondage. (3/9)*

> *Therefore, without being attached to the fruits of activities, one should act as a matter of duty, for by working without attachment one attains the Supreme. (3/19)*

> *And whoever, at the end of his life, quits this body, remembering Me alone, at once attains My nature. Of this there is no doubt. (8/5)*

To be able to put the above to practice, Arjuna has to pay heed to His following words of wisdom:

> *Because you are My very dear friend, I am speaking to you My supreme instruction, the most confidential knowledge of all. Hear this from Me, for it is for your benefit.*

> *Always think of Me, become My devotee, worship Me and offer your homage unto Me. Thus you will come to Me without fail. I promise you this because you are My very dear friend.*

Abandon all varieties of religion and just surrender unto Me. I shall deliver you from all sinful reactions. Do not fear. (18/64, 65 & 66).

In the final analysis, moving away from the immediate concerns of the Kurukshetra war, the Supreme Lord Krishna provides significant insight as to how He effectively controls all functions of this material cosmos and can thus be the true guiding spirit of today's CEOs for solving the current business problems as well as attain the ultimate salvation of the individual and the planet.

Chapter 6

Managing and Surviving Recession

After he reached his office in downtown Chicago one morning in September 2008, Rajan V. started to check his e-mails for the day. Soon he read one with horror that said he had lost his job. Devastated, he phoned his wife who told him that they had got a letter informing them about the foreclosure on their home. Now he had no job and no home. The news sites on his computer were full of the collapse of major banks and housing financing companies.

In the same week, K. Basu in London checked his portfolio and found that he had lost his fortune in the stocks he had invested in. His business was suffering because his losses were mounting due to low demand. Many shops had closed down on the main street of his suburb. If he could not pay his suppliers or his bank, he, too, would have to close down.

In Mumbai, Jayanti Patel did not know if he could keep his 150-odd employees making shirts as his export orders from Britain and the United States evaporated overnight. After the current consignment was shipped that week, he had no orders and wondered if this shipment would be paid by the overseas buyer. Even if he sacked his workers, he still had his factory to take care of and the bank overdraft to be repaid.

These three persons and thousands upon thousands of others the world over faced a bleak future for no fault of theirs with 'the Financial Tsunami' that hit the West and most countries in 2008. 'Buy, buy, buy' was the way to live it up for the preceding 20 years. In the United States, home loans were freely granted up to 120 per cent to cover even the legal costs! Cars and white goods came instantly on instalments that could start a year later. Credit cards seemed to grant unlimited credit. Demand boomed as the financial system created credit out of thin air. Since the crash of 1987, the stock markets rocketed and the good times got better and better. The spending spree stopped abruptly with this crash in 2008. Jobs vanished. Savings vapourized. Property prices plummeted. The 2008 global meltdown has rightly been compared to the Great Depression of 1929.

The 2008 global meltdown was a result of the free market system without enough controls on the financial system, especially in the United States. Thus, greed took over completely. So many people were making so much money that it seemed the good times would never end. For a start, high-priced homes were sold to Americans who could not pay their mortgages. So high property prices increased demand for homes and most products and services were sold on credit. These very risky loans were then re-branded. Some major American banks bundled these loans and separated the risk that these loans would turn sour from the risk from the loans themselves. This risk was sold to other financial companies that created bonds from them and sold them to investors. These investors were major banks in the US, Europe and many other countries. Credit risk was removed from banks on a massive scale. Like a speeding car with a drunk driver, the people who were supposed to regulate the financial system let it gather speed before it crashed. When the homeowners defaulted, the credit bubble burst in the US.

The 'Financial Tsunami' initially hit the West and later the world economy had a ripple effect all over the global financial system. The so-called financial wizards of the modern economy have been periodically devising different strategies, manipulating various aspects of fiscal system to achieve and maintain an unhealthy monetary situation. This resulted in a hollow boom throughout the world. Since the rest of the world exported to the United States and Europe, they were badly affected. India and China suffered but they had not invested heavily in bonds and so they recovered within a year by releasing billions for boosting and building their economies.

This financial hurricane has fully exposed the hollow intelligence of the so-called economic pundits who graduated from famous universities and managed the financial system. Even after many years, these so-called experts have neither any ready answers nor an immediate resolution for the acute problems we are facing. The worst affected are the most advanced countries of the West—USA, Britain and Europe. This ignominious failure of the modern economy has triggered a chain reaction. Stock markets have tumbled, banks have collapsed and many have been thrown out of jobs in countries round the globe. In early 2014, the US economy was showing signs of recovery, Britain was still struggling with its economic slowdown and European countries especially Greece, Italy, Portugal and Spain had suffered severe economic problems. Germany had bailed out Greece and other countries with huge loans through the European Union. However, the emerging economies of China and India with more government control of their banks and financial system recovered with less damage.

Can Financial Institutions be Trusted?

How can we trust any financial institution anymore? In the West, the share markets and the banking system have been assuring us full security of the hard-earned money of the blue and white collar workers as well as businessmen, deposited or invested with them. But they crashed and thousands of Americans were thrown out of their homes, lost their savings on the exchange and even their jobs. The average investor/depositor has become more anxious about the market fluctuation level than about his/her blood pressure and glucose levels.

The 2008 global meltdown is the result of uncontrolled greed. The Supreme Lord Krishna in the *Gita* (Ch 16 -21), identifies three gates leading to hell and one of them is greed.

Greed

A lavish lifestyle requires a constant supply of various objects and services of enjoyment and this arouses greed in a person. The intelligence of a greedy person will always devise novel means for amassing wealth. He bounces from one fruitless programme to another and never tires. He adopts illegal means and despite high political connections he may sometimes undergo imprisonment. This brings his family into disrepute. The family members also suffer due to his way of living. He is always tensed up and spends sleepless nights. Pouring of buckets of *ghee* into fire does not diminish the fire, rather starts to blaze. Similarly, impelled by greed, one's endeavour for earning more only increases the desire and never satiates it.

A greedy person accumulates a large quantity of money with great struggle and pains and may sometimes have no time to even eat his meals or take his family out on a holiday. He fools himself and others by thinking wrongly of themselves as *karma-yogis*. The following verse of the *Shrimad Bhagavatam* (11-23-16) makes an appropriate comment in this connection:

> *Whatever pure fame is possessed by the famous and whatever praiseworthy qualities are found in the virtuous are destroyed by even a small amount of greed, just as one's attractive physical beauty is ruined by a trace of white leprosy.*

A greedy man is just like a honey-bee who struggles to produce a large quantity of honey which is then stolen by a person who will enjoy it personally or sell it to others. One may argue that a wealthy man may conceal his money very expertly but no matter how carefully he hides his hard-earned wealth, there are those who are experts in detecting the whereabouts of valuable things and steal them.

Generally, a person becomes trapped under the burden of unnecessary material accumulation. Sometimes children of wealthy persons are kidnapped and the parents are compelled to pay huge ransoms. Many a time filthy-rich persons themselves become the target. We do not understand that we cannot become content even if we get all the property in the entire world. Finally, the Supreme Lord Krishna says in the *Gita* (10/34), 'In the form of death I take away everything'.

The best way to control greed is to give money in charity to devotees genuinely engaged in the propagation of Krishna consciousness. Otherwise, a rich man, while living, may lose a sizeable portion of his wealth in surprise income-tax raids or when diseased hospitals and medical practitioners will fleece him. After death when his sons will start quarrelling, and each one try to grab a larger share of the bequeathed wealth, the lawyers will gain immensely.

In addition to their huge pay cheques, the investment bankers in the West were getting multi-million bonuses every year for a number of years up to 2008. They wanted more. So they created these 'toxic' investments that blew up the financial system.

For a spiritually liberated person, the recent crisis is no surprise at all because with all the deceptively projected economic progress, he can clearly see the ground reality telling a different story. According to Indian history, during the times of *The Mahabharata*, over five thousand years ago, people ate out of golden plates and drank beverages from silver cups. Now we use paper plates for eating and plastic cups for drinking. Is this the sign of progress?

The very method of monetary transactions is based on false premises and a flawed system. The introduction of paper currency is the main defect of the system. In Vedic civilization, people acquired life's necessities on a barter basis by exchanging commodities without the use of money. Gold, silver, bronze, pearls, gems were considered wealth. Even today, these are real wealth and not the currency notes. Although the head of the banking system declares in every currency note that *'I promise to pay...'* we cannot trust this promise any more when it loses its value due to inflation and economic and political policies.

Since the world cannot go back to the barter system, we should handle money as if it belongs to the Supreme Lord Krishna. This will mean less attachment to money and all it can buy. By reducing our demands and living a simple lifestyle, we can reduce our dependence on money. Going back to the basic and time-honoured investments in the precious metals such as gold and silver—the prices of which have risen to record levels after this global meltdown—can provide better security. Of course, the real security is the Supreme Lord Krishna. No lesser person can give us security, not even the other heavenly Gods. The *Mahabharata* has many examples as presented in this book. The *Shrimad Bhagavatam* stresses the same point when Prahlada Maharaja prays to Narasimhadeva, an incarnation of Lord Krishna:

> *Oh My Supreme Lord Nrisimhadeva! Because of a bodily conception of life, embodied souls neglected and not cared for by you cannot do anything for their betterment. Whatever remedies they accept, although perhaps temporarily beneficial, are impermanent.*
>
> *(Shrimad Bhagavatam 7-9-19)*

For example, a father and a mother cannot protect their child, a physician and some medicine cannot relieve a suffering patient and a boat on the ocean cannot protect a drowning man. Even in the presence of parents, a child can die of an accident. A very rich man who is very sick may get admitted into the world's best hospital and consult expert physicians by paying high fees but none of these can save him from his impending death. Passengers thrown in mid-ocean from a drowning ship may get on to a boat bobbing nearby but before they can heave a sigh of relief, the boat may capsize by an unexpected wave, killing all of them. Thus, God alone is the real saviour.

The Saint, Narada Muni, enlightens Yudishthira on how no one else of this world, except God, can assure foolproof protection:

> *This gross material body made of five elements is already under the control of eternal time (kala), action (karma) and the modes of material nature (guna). How, then, can it, being already in the jaws of the serpent, protect others?*
>
> *(Shrimad Bhagavatam 1-13-46)*

Naradji is trying to drive home the point that the position of every living being is that of a person caught in the jaws of a serpent. How can such a person provide security to others? Everyone suffers or enjoys in this world according to the result of one's *karma* or action performed in previous lifetimes. Hence, sometimes we see that a person may perform good deeds in his life but is harassed by continuous miseries. Bewildered, he may even be sometimes tempted to stray away from the path of righteousness.

What Affects Our Moods

All of us are subjected to the influence of the modes of material nature, *guna*, *sattva*-goodness, *rajah* (passion) and *tamah* (ignorance). Our moods, behaviour, thoughts and mindset are all affected by this. None can escape from its effect within this whole universe, including various planetary rulers. Above these two is the time element, *kala*, which controls all the activities within the universe. No one, including the heavenly gods, can escape the onslaught of the great factor called time. Time is the impersonal aspect of the Supreme Lord Krishna. If none of us can save ourselves from the assault of eternal time, then how can any one of us provide security to others?

Everlasting security...this very idea is foolish because eventually everyone has to die. When we talk of security, the notion implies safety of the body. But when we die, the body has to be given up along with our very dear relatives and objects whether we like it or not. That is the law of nature. Rebuking Arjuna for his fallacious arguments and enabling him to realize this undeniable fact, the Lord says in the *Gita* (2/27), '*For one who has taken birth, death is certain*'. This means no one can exist for ever on this earth. Then, what everlasting security are we talking about?

The Real Investment

The real investment for our time, effort and energy is to discover our real self. *Vedanta*, the scripture that embodies the final conclusions of the ancient teachings, makes it clear in its very first *sutra* or aphorism. It says, '*Thereafter, therefore, enquire about Brahman or god*'. 'Thereafter' means that the evolving soul of this universe, after roaming the whole universe through various species of life, has now acquired a human body. 'Therefore' indicates that because the living entity has taken human birth, its only objective should be to enquire about the nature of the Absolute Transcendental Truth or God. Compared to birds and animals, human beings are endowed with sufficient intelligence and energy to enquire, investigate and realize their true identity as well as the ultimate source, God. To know God and our eternal relationship with Him is the only task of all human beings. If devoted to this aim and activity, our time and energy are well spent.

Whether we act piously or impiously in this world, it is meaningless in the ultimate sense. Any material actions performed here will oblige us to come back here after death to enjoy or suffer good or bad results in a new body, according to the concept of reincarnation. This means we have to take birth again, grow old, become diseased and ultimately die again. This will go on repeatedly. Therefore, the intelligent way of investing our time and effort is to seek a solution to put a stop to this cycle of repetitive birth and death. The Supreme Lord Krishna enlightens us in this connection in the *Gita* as follows:

> *One who knows the transcendental nature of My appearance and activities does not, upon leaving the body, take his birth again in this material world, but attains My eternal abode, O Arjuna.* (4/9)

And whoever, at the time of death, quits his body, remembering Me alone, at once attains My nature. Of this there is no doubt. (8/5)

After attaining Me, the great souls, who are yogis in devotion, never return to this temporary world,
that is full of miseries, because they have attained the highest perfection. (8/15)

From the highest planet in the material world down to the lowest, all are places of misery wherein repeated birth and death take place. But one who attains to My abode, O Son of Kunti, never takes birth again. (8/16)

What other way is there to invest our time and effort besides following Krishna's recommendation fruitfully?

The aftermath of the global meltdown means that we have to adjust to a lower standard of living by reducing our demands for comforts and luxuries we have become used to. Once the basic needs of food, clothing, housing and other services like education, health and transport are taken care of, we should know where to draw the line in our consumption. We can recall the plight of the former President of Iraq, Saddam Hussein. He built many grand palaces in which he originally lived but after the American invasion, he was forced to abandon them all and live, in the last stage of his life, in a hole below the earth, like a snake or a mouse.

Due to a false sense of security and an imaginary sense of enjoyment, catering to the aggravated sensual appetites, we have unnecessarily raised our standard of living to an artificial level in a competitive spirit. We have to give up the mindset of false prestige and unnaturally acquired social status. We should revert to simple living and high thinking. Whether the president of a nation or a pilot, a cobbler or a computer operator, we should always remember that we are basically servants of the Supreme Lord Krishna. This is our original and eternal status. This will help us to cope with any downsizing.

Living without Luxuries

How can we live without luxuries that all of us have got used to? In India, the scriptures of the *Ramayana* and the *Mahabharata* have many examples. In the *Ramayana*, Lord Ramachandra instantly gave up his luxurious palace life and lived like a mendicant in the forest for fourteen years. His chaste consort Sita, too, despite being a young married woman, endured all the rigours and dangers of the forest life. The other famous epic, the *Mahabharata*, also tells us that the five Pandava princes gave up all luxuries of their palace and lived in exile in the forest, suffering many hardships, for twelve years.

All these godly personalities can be our ideals. If we have truly accepted them as such, we are now required to follow in their footsteps. Then where is the problem for us to reconcile to the idea of a simple life? Our offices, homes, cars, shopping complexes and malls are all air-conditioned or centrally heated to provide comfort to our bodies. But, the fact is that this very body is buried under the earth or burnt by fire when we die. What is the problem in understanding this? The property owners generally claim that they own acres of land. This is an illusion because when they die, whether they are buried or cremated, the remains of the body mix with the earth. This means the land owns us and not vice versa. What more clarity do we need to understand our actual status? The Supreme Lord Krishna makes this point in the *Gita*:

An intelligent person does not take part in the sources of misery, which are due to contact with the material senses. O son of Kunti, such pleasures have a beginning and an end, and so the wise man does not delight in them. (5/22)

In this world of duality of delusion, nothing comes by itself. We may entertain the best hopes but should prepare ourselves for disappointments. The good is always accompanied by the bad, and sorrow closely follows happiness. After achievements, we may encounter failures. One may try very hard, clamouring for pleasures, but pain comes without seeking. Therefore, you should not become egoistic due to your exalted lineage, erudite scholarship, material opulence or handsome physique. Once we understand, imbibe and assimilate the truth about the illusory designations of this world, we can live peacefully in any situation.

As spirit souls, we are fragments of the Supreme Lord Krishna. Our body is composed of the five material elements: Earth, Water, Fire, Air and Ether, which are the components of the Lord's material energy. Thus, we owe our whole existence to the Supreme Lord Krishna. With this understanding, we should surrender and serve the Lord with love. This is our most secure investment.

The Supreme Lord Krishna's other name is Hrishikesha. *Hrishika* means senses and *'isha'* means controller. This means that the Supreme Lord Krishna is the controller of all our senses. Hence, offering loving devotional service to Krishna through our senses is called *bhakti, hrishikena Hrishikesha sevanam bhaktiriti uchyate.* We are unhappy because we are trying to engage our senses for our personal gratification.

After explaining all issues precisely and concisely in the battlefield of Kurukshetra, the Lord, at the end of the discourse in the *Gita*, left it to Arjuna to deliberate on the details and take a final decision about what he wanted to do. A friend and devotee of the Lord that he is, Arjuna responded by saying, 'I shall execute all your instructions'. This is called *sharanagati* or total surrender. Appreciating this, Krishna spoke assuringly as follows in the *Gita*:

> *Abandon all varieties of religion and just surrender unto Me. I shall deliver you from all the sinful reactions. Do not fear. (18/66)*

Through Arjuna, the Supreme Lord Krishna gives His ultimate advice to all of us when the Lord says: '*Give up all your imaginary sense of duty, responsibility and obligations based on bodily concept of life and take exclusive refuge in Me*'. This is the final guarantee. This is the real security. No other person in both the material and/or spiritual world can give such an assurance. For such a fully surrendered devotee, the Supreme Lord Krishna says: '*I shall take care of you. I shall even save you from the effect of all your sins*'. The Supreme Lord Krishna is also known as *Achyuta*, the infallible. He never fails in His commitment or in fulfilling the desire of His fully surrendered devotees. He never fails. This means that such devotees need not worry for their sustenance and protection. Shunning all the other superficial material activities, working exclusively for the Supreme Lord Krishna is the most secure investment.

Today, I am eating from a simple plate. Tomorrow, if I start eating from a silver plate, people will say 'I am advanced'. Why is that? The activity of eating is the same, whatever be the quality of the plate from which I eat. Similarly, we think that eating and mating are the highest forms of happiness. A hog that eats garbage and copulates is also happy with these activities. Then, how can we claim that we are more advanced than animals? The real advancement is spiritual advancement. We should know that the driver is different from the car he drives. We keep cleaning the car regularly but neglect the driver. We maintain our body with great attention and care but have no knowledge about the soul. Then, how are we advanced? The cage may be clean or dirty but the bird inside it must be fed properly. This is true advancement. Those who do not clearly understand the difference between the body and the soul think falsely that they are identical and that can find perfect happiness by gratifying their five physical senses. Hence, we hanker blindly for the enjoyment of our physical senses without making any effort to understand the real spiritual being.

Returns and Dividends

All human beings are always keen to build beautiful homes to live in and enjoy in luxury. But the result is ultimately fruitless and miserable. It is like fat rats. A rat is normally seen working hard to dig a big hole in the ground to live in it comfortably. But, invariably, a large, poisonous snake swallows the rat and enters into the hole strenuously dug up by the rat to stay there. Similarly, a man who is very much attached to his body toils very hard throughout his life, facing many obstacles, disappointments, failures and bottlenecks just to accumulate as much money as possible and build a huge home. He undergoes this great struggle to increase and provide security to his wife, children, grandchildren, relatives, friends, servants, and others. But, he may not live to enjoy these luxuries and wealth. He dies leaving all his belongings earned through many sufferings to be enjoyed by the so-called loving family members with whom he may be quarrelling or have no connection at all even before or after his death. He meets the fate of the fat rat.

It is common knowledge that an intelligent investor would always like to know what returns he is likely to obtain from an investment. When one works exclusively for the Supreme Lord Krishna, as in the case of Arjuna, the dividend is that he will be victorious in his efforts on this earth and also move away from the cycle of birth-death-birth and never return to this material world of miseries. Therefore, to cultivate Krishna Consciousness is the most secure investment.

Depressed in this Meltdown

Generally, only in times of distress does one think of God. It is, therefore, said that even '*Adversity is the benediction of God*'. Instead of becoming depressed, which will not serve any useful purpose, one must find time to reflect on the Supreme Lord Krishna and His essential teachings in the *Gita*. This will bring solace, and I will be small. We need to understand fully the deeper significance and implications of the Lord's insight as in the *Gita* (8/15), 'After attaining Me, the great souls, who are yogis in devotion, never return to this temporary world, which is full of miseries, because they have attained highest perfection.' The Lord further states in the *Gita* (2/56), 'One who is not disturbed in mind even amidst the threefold miseries or elated when there is happiness, and who is free from attachment, fear and anger is called a sage of steady mind.'

Lord Krishna suggests in the *Gita* (18/65), 'Always think of Me,' and 'Become My devotee,' or 'Worship Me,' or 'Offer obeisances to Me.' This is a universal instruction. Anyone can follow this irrespective of one's religion or beliefs. In today's hectic lifestyle of delirious activities, the easiest way to implement this is to chant the holy names of the Lord:

Hare Krishna Hare Krishna,
Krishna Krishna Hare Hare,
Hare Rama Hare Rama,
Rama Rama Hare Hare.

The Supreme Lord Krishna is not different from His names. There are no hard and fast rules about the chanting of this Mahamantra nor any question of eligibility. No medicines of allopathy or homeopathy are required. It is only the Supreme Lord Krishna who can rescue us from all types of depression.

Chapter 7

Successful Executives Use It or Lose It

As senior executives, Steve Smith in New York and Rishi Joshi in New Delhi have the same lifestyles. Report to work at 9 sharp every day. Brief their secretaries about the day's priorities. Then plunge into a series of meetings, project reports, evaluations, consultations that go on and on. No time for lunch except a quick bite. Finish late in the evening. Rush to a cocktail or a party. Finally, collapse into bed totally exhausted. No time for their children or even their wives. Frequent local and foreign trips. After all, they work for the same multi-national corporation.

The Supreme Lord Krishna watches modern executives—and indeed everyone else for that matter!—as they sink deep into materialistic lifestyles, visiting plush shopping malls for impulsive purchases, frequenting glitzy restaurants for meals, and hopping continents for expensive holidays with their laptops and Smartphones that never disconnect them for their work. In this hectic life, most executives sink neck-deep in materialism by adopting a Western or 'modern' way of life. In the process, he or she loses track of the very goal of human life and is often adrift in the hurly burly of the fiercely competitive corporate world.

Take the example of these two seemingly successful executives—though many of their objectives have been realized and earned them acclaim and adulation, yet they are in the grip of a terrifying emptiness. The impact of stress on them is severe. By the time they realize it, it will have already taken its toll beyond any possibility of recovery. Life in the fast lane is lonely at the top of the corporate ladder. And they are alone to face all the tension and stress for the benefits of high income. Honestly, does this make any sense? Is it for this lifestyle that they made so many sacrifices in life? Is it for this existence that they endured those terrible hardships? Will they slow down only after a heart attack? When is it enough? Is there any more to life than building the corporation and ruining their lives? Are they chasing a mirage or lost in an illusion?

News of Wall Street executives indulging in excessive drinking, non-stop gambling and cavorting with call-girls have shocked people. . These orgies of enjoyment surpassed those of the Roman emperors, the royalty of Europe and the Maharajas of India. These executives spend thousands upon thousands of dollars in a single night on their various tupes of pleasures. Similar stories also surfaced about British executives working in London's Financial District. These people thought that their parties would never end and went on enjoying recklessly until the Global Financial Meltdown put a crashing end to it all.

Many executives work at such a frenetic pace that peace always evades them. Losing sight of the oasis, driven by their bottomless ambition, they foolishly chase mirages in the desert. In the endless cycle of birth and death, we are unsure of what form we may be forced to accept in the next birth. Human birth is very valuable. Use it or lose it.

Instead of gloating over our weaknesses for enjoying our physical senses like beasts and birds in our human birth, we should discreetly turn to ways of God realization. This life in a human body is too valuable an opportunity to be squandered in the rat race of material progress and the desire to reach the top at any cost. For a conditioned soul, striving in this material world, attaining a human body is a rare achievement. Although temporary, like that of a hog or dog, it is meaningful because it offers us the opportunity to realise the ultimate purpose of our existence to attain liberation. Thinking at this higher level, the executives can go to a superior and the only worthwhile goal, instead of getting stuck in the tedium of everyday life in the corporate world.

To escape from this grim reality, many exectuives develop an alternate personality as they also suffer from delusions of grandeur. With an imaginary digital personality, they start an account on social media and falsely present themselves as young, dashing and attractive men working in a glamorous job. Of course, all this is totally opposite from the dull reality of their routine job. But on the web chat rooms or on social media sites, they become their alter ego and tempt the opposite sex with their imaginary exploits. They romance with their digital girlfriends and live secret lives of passion and fantasy. They think they have physical relationships with these friends.

In other cases, executives start romantic affairs in their office with their secretaries or their colleagues since they spend most of their daytime with them. On official retreats or conferences in other locations, these liaisons blossom into torrid love affairs and later cause problems with their wives as they are too involved with their lovers.

One should not get too attached to physical relationships— this is one of the key insights of the *Gita*. The materialistic relationships of a husband, a wife, children, relatives and friends are just like the casual temporary association that we enjoy when we visit posh restaurants or popular tourist spots. On such outings, particularly during visits to foreign countries, one may meet people who appear to hold emotional appeal. In fact, such association is temporary and meaningless. Similarly, relationships of society, friendship and love are merely the play of *maya* or illusion. One should not be deluded by material connections which initially blinkered Arjuna in the *Mahabharata*.

Stepping back from the corporate world, the effective executive realizes that he or she is not the body, but a spirit soul, part and parcel of the Supreme Lord Krishna. One begins to see that he or she has been entrapped somehow by material facades. True wisdom lies in disentangling oneself from this *mayik situation* and attaining liberation. Only those living beings with a human embodiment can start on this path. This is our challenge: Use it or lose it.

In single-minded devotion lies the answer. In an elaborate explanation of devotional service (Bhakti Yoga) to His friend Uddhava, the Supreme Lord Krishna concludes with this powerful command in *Shrimad Bhagavatam*: 'This process is the intelligence of the intelligent and the cleverness of the most clever, for by following it one can in this very life make use of the temporary and unreal to achieve Me, the eternal reality.'

Need to Step Back

The need to step back from materialism and embrace the path of the spirit is a realization that often sets in with advancing age. As the *Gita* says, nobody can stay in this world permanently. Everyone has to go: *adya, va abda shatanto va*, either today or at the end of one hundred years of age, die one must. There is no escape. Caught up in consumerism and materialism, one forgets that one is a mere mortal whose body is made of material elements. Because of its nature, it is referred to as *anrita*, false. Therefore, if one is truly intelligent—and this does not mean just meeting corporate deadlines or monthly performance charts, but in the sense of spiritual quotient, one should utilize this opportunity to attain *amrita*, the eternal reality or Krishna, the Supreme Lord..

This is where human beings differ from other species. While the bodies of animals and birds are also made of the same five material elements, the major difference is that human beings are empowered with extraordinary intelligence and a highly evolved consciousness to comprehend the real goal of life. Thus, only human beings are blessed with a chance to extricate themselves from material entrapment. Use it or lose it.

As the Supreme Lord Krishna says in the *Bhagavad Gita*, pleasure born of sensual contact is actually a source of misery. Any effort without a focus and single-mindedness is also doomed to failure. A person has to go through many hurdles to achieve a desired object. When he gets it, sub-consciously he fears its loss. When it is really lost, he falls apart completely. Many executives face this personal crisis when they lose their positions or jobs. The Supreme Lord Krishna has many valuable lessons for executives as He and Arjuna engage in a dialogue on how to maintain equilibrium in the face of challenges. The Supreme Lord Krishna shows Arjuna a clear way out of his morass of self-doubt by following the path of devotion or *bhakti*.

The Supreme Lord Krishna outlines three different paths in the *Gita*. They are nothing but progressive stages that necessarily culminate in Bhakti. The varied processes like *karma*, *jnana*, *dhyana* form a part of bhakti, and their goals do not exist separately. *Nishkama karma yoga* or effort without hankering for its reward but offering it to the Supreme Lord Krishna is for those whose minds are impure with innumerable worldly desires. *Jnana yoga* or the intellectual approach is suitable for those whose minds are free from material enjoying propensities. Those having theoretical, spiritual knowledge, after becoming free from material contamination, are qualified for a life of Jnana yoga. When pursued further, this leads one to the final stage of bhakti yoga, the transcendental loving devotional service to the Supreme Lord.

When exasperated, the executive could turn to the Supreme Lord Krishna for his answers in the *Gita* for creative problem-solving. The scripture offers insights into independently created solutions as it gives Arjuna a chance to think through the hurdles that plague him and work towards greater effectiveness and efficiency. It contains the need for clear plans, organizational skills and a corporate ambience of commitment and innovation but always with the inner commitment for Bhakti yoga that will ensure balance and lead to salvation of the soul.

Biggest Financial Scam

Materialism can never be the answer, says the Supreme Lord in the *Gita*. In his pursuit of material luxuries and money powered by greed, a former commissioner of New York Exchange, NASDAQ, Bernard 'Bernie' Madoff, ran a dishonest investment fund that cheated investors as much as $50 billion in what is called a 'Ponzi' scheme. In this scheme, the money from new investors is paid as high returns to existing investors. No investments are made, no profits are earned. The high returns for investors attract more money. Madoff pulled off this scam for over 25-30 years and amassed luxury homes, a boat, cars and every other luxury for himself and his wife. He went on cheating until March 2009 when many of his investors wanted their money back, and he was caught out and imprisoned. After his trial, he was jailed for 150 years in June 2009.

It became 'the largest investment fraud in Wall Street's history'. Where is the end of greed? What is the real goal of life?

The Supreme Lord guides us for the goal of *Brahma saukhyam tu anantam* or eternal unending happiness of the spiritual realm. The grim determination to climb the corporate ladder will not bring enduring happiness. Driven by ambition, many people are consumed by needless and sometimes imaginary anxieties due to lack of faith in the Divine. Obsessed with attaining results, they cannot find any solace and each step forward saps them of energy, physical strength and mental tranquillity. When blessed with our human form, we can use it for God realization. We either use it or lose it.

We brand a person as 'selfish' or 'self-centred' when he concentrates on his own well-being. He who also looks after the interests of his family members may look like a selfless person but actually he is not, because he attends to the needs of his own family and not of others. Similarly, one who lends all possible support to the advancement of his entire community also cannot be considered selfless because all that he does is for his own and not for other communities.

We generally come across wealthy men of various communities giving generous financial donations for social welfare projects like building schools, colleges, clinics and so on for the benefit of the communities to which they belong but not for communities that are not their own. A national social worker whose attitude transcends his family's and community's connections, toils hard for the prosperity of the whole nation is also considered selfish for he does everything for the sake of his own country and not of others. A global worker, though working for the good of the entire humanity, too, cannot escape the blemish of being selfish because all his attempts are made on the basis of bodily conception of life, expecting something in return like national or international posts or honours.

When you have the understanding that '*I am the body*', you cannot but be selfish. There are two kinds of selfishness: concentrated selfishness and extended selfishness. Concentrated selfishness refers to being concerned with your own personal needs while extended selfishness includes your family, society, community and nation. The first one is generally observed in animal society and the second is seen in human society. Sense enjoyment is the root cause of this selfishness. Here again there are two types: gross physical body sense enjoyment and subtle body gratification. Gross physical body enjoyment is experienced through the five senses of taste, smell, hearing, touching, and seeing. This happens as in eating, sleeping, defending and mating. Subtle body which comprises mainly mind and intelligence, hankers after gratification through gaining fame, prestige and adoration.

A Selfish Motive

In other words, there is only a selfish motive in whatever one does as long as he or she suffers from illusory identification of body as self. That is precisely why corporate culture is dominated by back stabbing, jealousy, corruption, embezzlement of money and all other illicit and illegal activities. Political culture is even worse where murder is sometimes part of the gameplan. All this for a seat in the boardroom or a ministerial cabinet.

Subtle body sense gratification aiming at gaining recognition and honour in society is worse than physical sense gratification. People are ready to buy name and fame by paying money. They want to see their names and photographs in the newspaper, magazines, and in the electronic media. This urge for fame is so strong that they even try to cut down people who are more popular. The craving for fame is lethal. A twenty-year-old American student recently killed around fifteen persons in a supermarket and then killed himself, leaving a suicide note saying that he was doing that just to become famous. This is not an exceptional case but happens often in the United States where the hunger for short-lived fame is obsessive. In his craving for fame, he even failed to realize that he would not live to see the result of his action. Similarly, a wealthy man wrote in his will that inheritors of his property must set aside at least one million rupees for a grand funeral procession. Such is the nature of *pratishtha asha*, the urge for gaining adulation and adoration—even after death!

Suffering from the misconception that the body is the self, even Arjuna was initially hesitant to fight in the Kurukshetra war. This is also an indirect sense gratification. His initial refusal to fight was not due to compassion. He was wondering if all the relatives on both sides died in the war, what use is victory as no one would be left to share the joy of success. This is his mindset. That is why the Supreme Lord Krishna, at the beginning of the *Gita's* discourse, tried to enlighten him about his actual self being the spirit soul and not the body.

The great sage Vyasadeva, the author of the Vedas and Vedanta, condemns the bodily conception of life very strongly in the following verse from his work *Srimad Bhagavatam* (10-84-13): 'One who identifies his self as the inert body composed of mucus, bile and air, who assumes his wife and family are permanently his own, who thinks the land of his birth is worth worshipping, or who sees a place of pilgrimage as merely the water there, but who never identifies himself with, feels kinship with, worships or even visits those who are wise in spiritual truth—such a person is no better than an animal like a cow or an ass.'

This body is made of five elements, namely, earth, water, fire, air and ether according to the *Gita* (7/4). Here it is said *kunape tri dhatuke*. *Kunape* means leather bag. Our body is compared to a leather bag. This leather bag consists of three elements, mucus, bile and air. An unbalance in their proportion causes diseases of the body which, when neglected, results in death.

One should not be very much attached to one's body. Thinking of oneself an Indian, American, French or even a man and a woman is ignorance in the final analysis. When an Indian dies, there is no guarantee that he will be born again in India. Therefore, it is foolish to claim to belong to a particular nationality or race. One may not even be born as a human being. Similarly, it is foolish to consider a wife, children or relatives as one's own. One who does not understand this truth is called '*go kharah*' or an animal.

Not Happiness but Distress

The material world does provide happiness, but distress, with every happiness, also comes as its companion. Although everyone is struggling very hard purely for attaining happiness, distress comes periodically without any invitation. Corporate executives are working almost non-stop all day and night, trying to increase their material status for enjoying more physical comforts and ego boosters. Suppose they attain these goals, yet the real problem of their lives is not solved. Where is peace for them? They forget that with the human body, they can also follow the path of the Supreme Lord Krishna and prosper in this world and also attain peace and ultimately liberation. They have the chance to use it or lose it.

Yet they work only for themselves and their immediate families. Since their minds and senses are uncontrolled, they become increasingly attached to family life. This is the big illusion. Providing comforts and luxuries for their families is their main goal. Animals like tigers, lions, elephants and crocodiles also provide food and protection to their young ones. Birds also fly very long distances to obtain food for the baby birds and build nests for their security. What is the major difference when human beings also act like animals claiming that they are duty-bound to do it? At the core of it all is greed to get more and more and provide more and more for their family by hook or by crook.

Thus, an ignorant living entity, inept at controlling the senses and mind, gradually becomes implicated in material activities, life after life. He is just like a silkworm that uses its saliva to create a cocoon and becomes trapped in it without any exit. A living being of this world becomes entangled in material result-oriented activities in the name of family, community and nation. This situation is described in Vedic literature as *adanta gobhih vishatam tamishram punah punah charvita charvananam*, because of their unbridled physical senses, persons too addicted to materialistic life slide down to a hellish condition and repeatedly chew what has already been chewed. What pleasure can one get in chewing a piece of sugarcane, spitting it out and picking it up again and chewing it repeatedly? Similarly, what pleasure can there be in taking birth as a child, going to school, attending college to obtain a degree, making money by doing a job or owning a business, getting married, producing children and grandchildren and ultimately dying only to take birth again to go through all these activities repeatedly?

The Root Cause

The root cause of this precarious situation is explained in *Shrimad Bhagavatam* (7-5-31) as: 'Persons who are strongly entrapped by the consciousness of enjoying material life, and who have, therefore, accepted as their leader or guru a similar blind man attached to external sense objects, cannot understand that the goal of life is to return home, back to Godhead, and engage in the service of Lord Vishnu. As blind men guided by another blind man miss the right path and fall into a ditch, materially attached men led by other materially attached men are bound by the ropes of fruitive labour, which are made of very strong chords, and they continue again and again in materialistic life, suffering the threefold miseries.'

The three-fold miseries are: first, *adhyatmika*, mental depression and gross physical illness; second, *adhibhautika*, suffering caused by other living beings starting from mosquito bite to terrorist attacks; and third, *adhi daivika*, natural calamities like earthquake, famine and floods. Does anyone, educated or uneducated, rich or poor, have any immunity against these three types of miseries? Can the so-called self-improvement programmes assure anyone total insulation from these? Therefore, an intelligent man must seriously inquire about the root cause of all these and how to ensure foolproof security against these.

The fact is that *na te viduh*—they do not understand. One may be an Oxford graduate, a billionaire businessman, an executive head of a powerful nation or a successful professional, yet the scripture maintains that they do not understand. What do they not understand? Their *svartha-gatim*, real self-interest. In other words, selfishness is not realized by them.

Actual Self Interest

What is actual self-interest? It is *Vishnu*, the Supreme Lord Vishnu or Lord Krishna. In Sanskrit,*Vishnu* means all-pervasive. Lord Vishnu pervades the entire universe by His impersonal feature. He is even in every atom. There is no moving or non-moving entity in this world without His presence. In the *Gita* (10/21), the Supreme Lord Krishna says *adityanam aham Vishnu, I am Vishnu among the sons of* Aditi. Hence, the Supreme Lord Krishna is the original Vishnu. Thus, Krishna Consciousness is our actual self-interest. This people engrossed in material consciousness do not understand. It is not merely the general masses that do not understand but even great learned scholars and leaders of the society lack this knowledge. They are, therefore, guilty of being blind and leading the blind. Hence if a blind person walking on a dangerous path is to be saved and be directed towards the right way, then, a person with proper sight is required.

At the beginning of the battle of Kurukshetra, Arjuna, the recipient of the *Bhagavat Gita* discourse, was also ignorant. He did not know the real goal of life, his true self-interest. The Supreme Lord Krishna impresses upon him that, *kshetra-kshetragnayor jnanam yat tat jnanam matam mama, to understand body and its owner is called knowledge. This is my opinion.* (*Gita* 13/2)

Kshetra means body and *Kshetrajna* means knower of the body, that is, the spirit soul or *Jivatma*. The Supreme Lord Krishna informs Arjuna that He also dwells in the heart of all living beings as the super soul *Paramatma* along with the individual soul. Hence, the knowledge of the body, *jivatma*, the individual owner of the body and the super soul *Paramatma* is called perfect spiritual knowledge. Only by the grace of the super soul can the individual soul become the knower of the distinction between himself and the body in a complete sense. Only by the Supreme Lord Krishna's grace can we know that the real purpose of the human body is to achieve self-realization and God realization.

What is the way to gain this understanding? *Shrimad Bhagavatam* (11-3-21) gives us the direction. It says: *tasmat gurum prapadyeta jijnasu shreya uttamam.* It means: 'Therefore a person who is seriously inclined to know about the real self-interest must seek a *bona fide* spiritual master, take shelter under his guidance after initiation'. We should not just approach any so-called guru for this purpose. The qualities of a *bona fide* spiritual master or Acharya are: first, he has realized the essential conclusion of the scriptures; second, he lives twenty-four hours with full surrender and service in Krishna Consciousness. Only such a *bona fide* Acharya is fully aware of actual self-interest.

Only human beings have the option to start on this journey of self-realization under an Acharya. Beasts and birds do not. So the corporate executive can either continue with his materialistic life with all its tensions and stress to lose his peace and balance. Or, he can surrender to the Supreme Lord Krishna and work selflessly without hankering for rewards. This is his choice to use it or lose it.

Chapter 8

The Ultimate Management Guru

'How can the Bhagavad Gita become a management textbook?' wondered Kavita Bhardwaj, studying for a management degree at an American university, after reading some recent references to the Gita as a management treatise. In India, she saw her grandmother reading the holy book every morning and was brought up to believe that it was a purely religious scripture. Now she is told of a new role for this holy text. While surfing the net, she came across hundreds of references on 'The Gita and Management'. A recent term 'Karma Capitalism' also mentioned the Gita. 'How did it all fit in?' she wondered.

These management theories ranged from academic research papers for management journals to leading articles in top magazines like *Business Week*. There were quite a few full-length books written on this topic, she discovered. More interestingly, she found that several major corporations in India and a few in the West were actually reading this ancient text, while several leading management gurus, captains of business and industry in India reported that reading the *Gita* and implementing its principles helped them to overcome crises that could have sunk their companies.

While lecturing at different universities in the United States, such as George Washington, University of Massachusetts, University of Maryland, and others, and at Oxford and Cambridge in Britain, many students often ask me: 'Can we learn any lessons for our careers from Lord Krishna?'

My simple response is that the entire life of the Supreme Lord Krishna is a wonderful lesson for your career today as a self-employed professional, a corporate executive, a CEO or even as the owner of a large enterprise. Many B-Schools in India and a few abroad are now including the teachings of the Supreme Lord Krishna in the *Gita* as part of their curriculum. Leading management experts and authors in India and the United States regularly mention the *Gita* as an important management text with practical lessons. Management trainers include insights from the *Gita* in their high-powered training programmes.

One of the leading business magazines of the world, *Business Week*, published from New York, carried an article 'Karma Capitalism' in its issue of 30 October 2006, pointing out that the *Gita* had replaced *The Art of War* by the Chinese military strategist, Sun Tzu. The article provided several examples of leading American B-Schools teaching management lessons from the *Gita* and quoted a large number of leading authors and thinkers in the West endorsing the *Gita* as a management tool. (Karma capitalism and its relevance to Krishna Consciousness are examined in the appendix at the end of this chapter.)

The *Gita* has also drawn the attention of management experts and authors in the Far East. In January 2007, the Singapore Management Review published a paper by Dr Charles Chow Hoi Hee entitled 'A Holistic Approach to Business Management:

Perspectives from the Bhagavad Gita'. The author is the owner of the East-West Group, prior to which he worked as the manager of International Operations at Singapore Trade Development Board.

The author starts by listing the major components in business as the '5Cs': capital, capability, connections, communication and commitment. However, he adds that business thrives on truth and integrity. To bridge the gap between profit-centric and purpose-centric management, this paper extracts management wisdom from the *Gita*.

The author finds parallels with the world of business in the initial stages of the *Gita*, where Arjuna is overcome by self-doubt. He says that this crisis can be interpreted as a corporate executive paralysed when faced with decisive action. At the corporate level, it is equivalent to a situation where quantitative justification does not warrant embarking on a business project. But a decision needs to be taken for the long-term survival of the corporation. The selfless action advocated by the Supreme Lord Krishna can be viewed as a manager remaining at the cutting edge of niche competencies. It could also be seen as a necessity for lifelong learning. At the corporate level, it emphasizes social responsibility to share the fruits of labour with society at large. The *Gita* presents three courses of action. *Jnana yoga* is the key to detachment. This supreme truth is comparable to the manager's need for reality checks—being aware of one's resources and influences and working within one's limitations. For the company, this translates into the need for an analysis of SWOT: Strengths, Weaknesses, Opportunities and Threats.

Bhakti yoga too has its lesson for managers—the need to remain in grace through unconditional devotion. Thus, the Supreme Lord Krishna's wisdom on the Supreme Self, when applied to the manager, emphasises that his reputation precedes him and lingers on after his death. At the corporate level, this means developing brand value. These yogas aspire to link human beings with the Divine.

What about the THIRD yoga? How does it apply to management decisions?

There are basically four types of managers: *the conservatives* who believe in doing things right and resist change; *the entrepreneurs* who believe in doing the right thing by taking risks for new ventures and thrive on change; *the leaders* who represent change and also get others to do the right things; and *the politician* who complicates issues on doing the right thing and not annoying anyone, if possible. However, all these managers have to optimize their '5Cs' for profitability and productivity.

It is commendable that Dr. Charles Chow Hoi Hee was inspired by the *Gita* to produce a paper on its applications for management. The Supreme Lord Krishna told Arjuna in the *Gita* 4:3 that he was His devotee and friend and hence qualified to understand the real purport of His message. But Dr Charles Chow Hoi Hee is not a practising Krishna Conscious person and hence his understanding is limited. In an eagerness to show the relevance of the *Gita's* teaching for modern management, he has resorted to a skewed interpretation or probably relied on non-bona fide commentators. Thus he made misleading references.

The objective of modern business organizations is to maximize profits for its owners for their sense gratification. If a Krishna Conscious executive manages a business organization, the objective then turns towards self-realization and not self-gratification. Thus, the entire perspective of capital, capability, connection, communication, and most important, commitment, changes along the following lines.

Capital

Dr Charles Chow Hoi Hee: Capital comprises money, men, machines and methods. Core competencies, intellectual properties and niche expertise are intangible capital. However, the business motive is expressed in an unstinting business vision, mission and core values. The Supreme Lord Krishna says in the *Gita* (3:35):

> Nothing is ever lost in following one's own dharma, but competition in another's dharma breeds fear and insecurity.

Therefore, realizing one's contribution to the entire cluster or industry is vital in unifying and justifying one's existence.

Money, men, machines and materials are basically to be employed for profits, but these profits are to be offered to the Supreme Lord Krishna. The purport of the sloka 3:35 in the *Gita* is that one should capitalize on one's inherent qualities in performing his duties instead of imitating those of others whose natures differ, and realize one's true potential for self-realization. The purport is that in the corporate sector, too, duties must be assigned to all employees according to their innate nature so as to get optimum output from them. Thus one gradually evolves spiritually too.

For a transmigrating soul within the conditioned atmosphere of this material universe, acquiring a human body is as valuable as the capital with which it can gain eternal residence in the spiritual abode of Vaikuntha or Vrindavana.

Liberation from this world should be the basic aim of all those who have a human form, although engaged in secular duties. The Lord explains this in detail while advising on various subjects to the Lord's dear friend and devotee, Uddhava, in *Shrimad Bhagavatam* (11-20-17) as follows:

'The human body, which can award all benefits in life, is automatically obtained by the laws of nature, although it is a very rare achievement. This human body can be compared to a perfectly constructed boat having the spiritual teacher as the captain, the instructions of the Supreme Lord as favourable winds impelling it on its course. Considering all these advantages, a human being who does not utilize his human life to cross the ocean of material existence must be considered the killer of his own soul.'

The human body, gained after passing through many inferior forms of beasts, birds and plants, is created in such a way that it can reach the highest perfection of life which is self-realization. Anyone, who deliberately or due to his ignorance discards these facilities, is actually acting against his own self-interest, and gradually becomes a killer of his own soul.

In the translation of verse 3.35 of the *Gita*, the word 'competition' is inappropriate. The true meaning of this verse is:

It is far better to discharge one's prescribed duties, even though faultily, than another's duties perfectly. Destruction in the course of performing one's own duty is better than engaging in another's duties, for to follow another's path is dangerous.

Capability

Acording to Dr Charles Chow Hoi Hee, capability refers to the intrinsic qualities that contribute to competitive advantage, for instance, outsourcing, corporate governance and social responsibility. The Supreme Lord Krishna says in the *Gita*:

Reshape yourself through the power of your will; never let yourself be degraded by self-will. The will is the only friend of the Self, and the will is the only enemy of the Self.

This has no relevance. This specifically is an exhortation to disconnect yourself totally from material life and to attempt at liberation.

One's capability to achieve anything, first of all, stems from the mind. Psychological strength is the basis for executing difficult physical endeavours. Possessing a strong muscular body is no use for a mentally debilitated person. We have often seen in a circus that a strong bodied lion slavishly acts according to the direction of an emaciated skinny person. This is because fear has been infused in the mind of the lion. Hence, the physical capability of the lion is reduced to a very great extent.

Thus, when the Supreme Lord Krishna saw Arjuna as a psychologically weak person that rendered him physically incapable, to remove his misconception and to boost his morale, He spoke to Arjuna thus as recorded in the *Gita* (6/6):

'For him who has conquered the mind, the mind is the best of friends, but for one who has failed to do so, his mind will remain his greatest enemy.'

Connections

Dr Charles Chow Hoi Hee maintains that a business venture needs connections to capture its demand side. These include 'feed-forward' (market intelligence, feasibility studies) and feedback such as reviews and audits. In the *Gita*, there is the phrase: *Om, Tat, Sat. Om* is the sacred syllable that connects the known to the unknown;

Tat is the supreme reality beyond what human thoughts or language can describe; and *Sat* embodies all that is good in self-harmony. Being connected with these realities means staying afloat on the same boat.

This is a distorted translation. ***'OM'*** is pronounced for performing result-oriented work. ***'Tat'*** is pronounced for freeing oneself from reactions of work. ***'Sat'*** is pronounced for work performed for the pleasure of the Supreme Lord Krishna. This is the actual meaning of this verse. The Supreme Lord Krishna derides people who are ignorant of their eternal connections with Him and try to be happy independently. In the *Gita* (2:66), he says:

> *One who is disconnected from Me cannot have pure intelligence. Consequently such a person's thought flow will always remain polluted, due to inordinate material desires. A desiring mind is a disturbed mind and cannot experience peace. How can a person who lacks tranquillity be happy?*

One cannot become easily successful merely by hard work in any field including business. This is a known fact today. 'High connections' are certainly required at all levels of dealings to ensure trouble-free transactions, both local and global.

Lord Chaitanya Mahaprabhu revealed in His teachings that the Vedas contain three sections, namely, 'Sambandha' (Connection or relationship), 'Abhidheya' (duty to be performed based on the knowledge of such relationship) and 'Prayojana' (achieving the objective, that is the love of the person related to, that is, the love of God).

The Supreme Lord Krishna also warns Arjuna not to be over-anxious about his temporary bodily connections but to realize the need to understand his eternal relationship with the Supreme

Lord which alone can extricate him from the quagmire of material existence, which is the real problem. He says in the *Gita* (7/14):

'It is very difficult to free oneself from the influence of the My deluding potency. Only those who have re-established their eternal connections with Me through full surrender can escape from Maya's clutches.'

Communication

Dr Charles Chow Hoi Hee thinks that besides the sender and the receiver (worthy or unworthy), communication within the *Gita's* perspective is dependent on timing and circumstances, regardless of content and duration of the message. From the business perspective, data mining and market analyses help prepare effective strategies, plans, projects and deliveries to target audiences. The Supreme Lord Krishna provides numerous examples in the *Gita*.

In Vedic terms, communication is known as *amnaya*. Teachings handed down through an authoritative line of spiritual masters or gurus in a chain of disciples, is called *avaroha pantha* or the top-down method. While this traditional line of communication, also known as the *parampara* system, ensures the purity and originality of the message, it also retains the authority.

The Supreme Lord Krishna, being the ultimate spiritual master, is an impeccable communicator and systematically inculcated the science of the *Gita* by first imparting the knowledge to the Sun God. The personality of the Godhead, the Lord said in the *Gita* (4:1-2):

I instructed this imperishable science of yoga to the Sun God, Visvasvan, and Visvasvan instructed it to Manu, the father of mankind, and Manu in turn instructed it to Iksvaku (a king).

Effective communication is a vital aspect of any organization to ensure that the company's policies and objectives are properly imbibed, assimilated and implemented at the grassroot levels. A communication gap can sometimes result in harmful distortions and create havoc.

Commitment

Dr Charles Chow Hoi Hee writes that another purpose-centric perspective is the commitment of managers and owners to the business as an ongoing concern that the Lord makes clear in the *Gita*.

These considerations are then consolidated into a management policy which promotes decision-making based on urgency and priorities. Matters that are neither urgent nor important can be delegated. For urgent but unimportant issues, appropriate parties could be empowered to act. Likewise, matters that are not urgent but are important usually affect the business in the long term, requiring an extensive network of expertise. As for urgent and important matters, usually depicted in a crisis or chaotic situation, leadership is vital. Dr Charles Chow Hoi Hee breaks new ground when he uses the Supreme Lord Krishna's message to show managers and management students the way, as they climb up the corporate ladder, with all its trials and tribulations.

Commitment stems from loyalty and a sense of belonging to an organization. The result-oriented assessment based on 'kick the stool after it is over' or 'hire and fire' philosophy of modern corporate management can hardly inspire even a highly paid executive to remain committed to his allotted functions. Nor does an over-ambitious and a greedy corporate employee, motivated by a desire to make a 'fast buck', trying to hop from one organization to another, can show genuine commitment in his performances.

The Supreme Lord Krishna's sense of commitment is exemplary as can be seen by the His statements in the *Gita* (3:22-24):

> *O son of Prtha, there is no work prescribed for Me within all the three planetary systems. Nor am I in want of anything, nor have I a need to obtain anything – and yet I am engaged in prescribed duties.*
>
> *For if I ever failed to engage in carefully performing prescribed duties, O Partha, certainly all men would follow My path.*
>
> *If I did not perform prescribed duties, all of these worlds would be ruined. I would be the cause of creating unwanted population, and I would thereby destroy the peace of all living beings.*

Can One Manage Oneself?

A paper entitled 'Managerial Effectiveness from the Perspectives of the Bhagavad Gita' was presented by Balakrishnan Muniapan at the School of Business, Curtin University of Technology, Sarawak, Malaysia. A very popular article published on numerous websites was written by MP Bhattathiry, a retired Chief Technical Examiner of the Government of Kerala, entitled 'Bhagavad Gita and Management'. http://www.boloji.com/hinduism/073.htm.

As in the case of Dr Charles Chow Hoi Hee, Bhattathiry draws similar conclusions, as he is not a practising Krishna Conscious person. His interpretations and references made here are misleading.

MP Bhattathiry says that the critical question in every manager's mind is how to be effective in his job. He finds the answer to this fundamental question in the *Gita* which repeatedly proclaims that 'You should try to manage yourself'. In effect, says Bhattathiry, it means that the answer lies in the manager himself. Unless the manager reaches a level of excellence and effectiveness that sets him apart from the others whom he is managing, he will merely be a face in the crowd and not an achiever.

Nowhere in the *Gita* does the Supreme Lord Krishna say that one can manage oneself. The only path is to surrender to His bona fide representative. The very fact that a capable person like Arjuna lost composure shows that one cannot manage oneself without a proper direction from an authority. In the *Gita*, 4.34, it is said:

> Just try to learn the truth by approaching a spiritual master. Inquire from him submissively and render service unto him. The self-realized souls can impart knowledge unto you because they have seen the truth.

The Gita and Managerial Effectiveness

Bhattathiry re-examines some modern management concepts in the light of the *Bhagavad Gita* which he observes is a primer on management by values. The first lesson in management, 'Utilisation of Available Resources', is seen in the initial scene of the *Mahabharata*. Before the war begins, Duryodhana, the eldest of the hundred Kaurava brothers, chooses the Supreme Lord Krishna's large army to help him, while Arjuna, one of the five Pandava brothers, relies on His wisdom for support. From this episode, Bhattathiry infers that an effective manager needs to be able to make a wise decision and then make optimum use of the scarce resources available.

Work Commitment

Picking up the management concept of work commitment, the writer quotes the popular verse 2:47 of the *Gita* which exhorts us to work without expecting a reward.

MP Bhattathiry says, 'Work for the sake of work suffers.' Dedication to one's task or job is questionable if we are calculating the date of promotion. Such work, he argues, cannot be commitment-oriented or even produce excellence. Today's promotion-oriented jobs often result in inevitable disappointments. The other fall-out of this style of management, is psychological. While performing with the aim of anticipated benefits, the quality of performance suffers on account of mental anxieties for the future.

The *Gita* tells us not to mortgage present commitment to an uncertain future. The Supreme Lord Krishna told Arjuna to do his duty without thinking of the reward or end result. Similarly, a manager should 'work for the pleasure of doing great work,' and not with an eye fixed on promotions at the end of the year. A manager will produce extraordinary results if he takes pride in the work he does. This emphasis on self-esteem, commitment and pride in one's work, the enthusiasm to attain the seemingly unachievable, will prevent disappointments and early burnouts which are common in the present work-and-reward-oriented work culture, says Bhattathiry.

On the contrary, fighting for the sake of fighting, 'yuddhaya yujyasva', is the actual instruction contained in verse 2-38 of the *Gita*, of course, without being anxious for the result it may deliver. Everyone works only with the aim of enjoying the fruits. Whether a CEO or a sweeper, he or she will not work merely for the pleasure of doing it or taking pride in doing it. The very goal of a corporate worker is to go up in the hierarchal order and to earn more remuneration.

Actually, one should work for the pleasure of the Supreme Lord—and not for one's own pleasure because this impedes one's commitment. Working for the satisfaction of the Supreme Lord Krishna has no scope for selfish motive. The correct translation of the sloka 2-47 *Gita* is:

You have a right to perform your prescribed duty, but you are not entitled to the fruits of action. Never consider yourself the cause of the results of your activities, and never be attached to not doing your duty.

The Supreme Lord Krishna's beseeching Arjuna to engage in war if for no other purpose, but to show the world his work commitment. He says in the *Gita* (3/33),

'Even a man of knowledge acts according to his own nature, for everyone follows the nature he has acquired from the three modes. What can repression accomplish?'

The Supreme Lord highlights the importance of one's commitment to one's duty. Unless one is fully Krishna conscious, one should not give up one's occupational duties. No one should whimsically give up one's prescribed duties based on one's nature and become a pseudo yogi or sanyasi. But many people do because it brings them respect and money. It is better to remain in one's natural work position and practise bhakti yoga. In short, the Supreme Lord articulates that enlightened action is better than renunciation in ignorance.

Responsibility with Accountability

M.P. Bhattathiry points out that critics argue this very teaching *Gita*, that being unattached to the consequences of one's actions promotes unaccountability. But Bhattathiry counters this argument, saying that while the *Gita* teaches detachment to reward, in no way does it remove one from accountability. On the contrary, he says the *Gita* does not absolve anyone from the consequences of his actions. The Supreme Lord Krishna points out to Arjuna that he has not been accountable and has not performed his dharma which is to fight.

Responsibility, based on the delegation of authority, demands accountability. Many people think that *nishkarma yoga*, selfless work, with the results dedicated to the Supreme Lord, promotes fatalism and encourages escapism to avoid responsibility and accountability. This is not true. The Supreme Lord cites examples of ancient kings to emphasise the need for Arjuna to realize his accountability and responsibility as a renowned warrior and a highly respected royal of the Kaurava dynasty. The Lord points out in the *Gita* (3:20):

> *Kings such as Janaka attained perfection solely by performance of prescribed duties. Thus, for the sake of educating the people in general, you should perform your work.*

Job Satisfaction

M.P. Bhattathiry makes an interesting point about the Motivational Theory of Personal Management. Turning the theory on its head, he says that it has long been assumed that satisfying the basic needs of a worker such as adequate food, clothing and shelter, recognition, appreciation, status, personality development are the key factors of motivation. The list of grievances from the clerk to the director is identical, differing only in scale. If this were true, it should then follow that once these lower-order needs are satisfied, the director and the clerk should not have any problems in optimizing their contributions to the organization. But this does not normally happen. The disgruntled remain disgruntled. A low-paid schoolteacher, a self-employed artisan or a committed struggling artist demonstrate higher levels of satisfaction even when their basic needs are not well met. This is because, he reasons, they are able to understand the self-better, as ably explained in the *Gita*.

Only a Krishna Conscious person can get job satisfaction because he or she knows how to reduce the desires of the physical senses. A Krishna Conscious person will only accept what is absolutely essential to live a healthy life. Both the poverty-stricken *Sudama Brahmana* and the immensely affluent King Ambarisha derived job satisfaction because they perfectly executed their duties as *Brahmana* and *Kshatriya* respectively despite the difference in their economic status since they were in Krishna consciousness.

Whether you are a CEO or a factory worker, rich or poor, a man or a woman, every one of you can become self-realized, if you are serious about it and desire it intensely. What is required is intensity in desire to learn about the spiritual truth. Poverty or low income alone is not the qualification nor affluence or elite status a disqualification to grasp spiritual essence.

Who are Visionaries?

According to M.P. Bhattathiry, the theory of self-transcendence over self-realisation is propounded in the *Gita*. Self-transcendence means overcoming obstacles in one's path. It involves renouncing egoism, putting others before oneself, teamwork, dignity, sharing, cooperation, harmony, trust, sacrificing lower needs for higher goals. The portrait of a self-realising person is one who aims at his own position and underrates everything else. On the other hand, the self-transcenders are the visionaries and innovators. Their resolute efforts enable them to achieve the apparently impossible. They overcome all barriers to reach their goal. Rather than a Theory of Motivation, Bhattathiry suggests that present-day organizations should create a culture which inculcates a Theory of Inspiration.

'*Obstacles in one's path*' is a wrong interpretation of self-transcendence. 'A self-realizing person aiming at his own position' is again an imaginary concept. Both these are misleading and incorrect explanations. The *Gita* certainly does not speak of these. Visionaries are those who have clear foresight who can make flawless forecasts of things to come. In Sanskrit, they are called 'Rishis'. *Pashyate iti rishi*, one who can foresee is a 'rishi' whereas '*manute iti muni*', one who speculates is a 'muni'. Great saintly personalities such as Narada, Veda Vyasa and Valmiki are known as Maharishis—great seers.

The Supreme Lord Krishna is the greatest visionary. This is because while great sages of the past cultivated a mystic ability to foresee through the penances and austerities, all the mystic powers have their source in the Lord. The Lord's assertiveness in this regard finds expression in the following verse of the *Gita* (7/26):

> *'O Arjuna, as the Supreme Personality of Godhead, I know everything that has happened in the past, all that is happening in the present, and all the things that are yet to come. I also know all living entities; but me no one knows.'*

The Supreme Lord could easily visualize the result of the war. He helped Arjuna to have a glimpse of what was to follow by revealing His Vishwarupa or Universal Form. The Supreme Lord also warned Arjuna in the *Gita* (18/58):

> *'If you become conscious of Me, you will pass over all the obstacles of conditioned life by My grace. If, however, you do not work in such consciousness but act through false ego, not hearing Me, you will be lost.'*

Finally the Supreme Lord Krishna, the greatest visionary, instructed Arjuna without mincing any word to surrender unto Him totally for his own benefit. He further speaks the following to Arjuna in the *Gita* (18/65):

'Always think of Me, become My devotee, worship Me, and offer your homage unto Me. Thus you will come to Me without fail. I promise you this because you are My very dear friend.'

Work Culture: Work is Worship

MP Bhattathiry claims that work culture means continuous effort in pursuit of a given or a chosen task. The Supreme Lord Krishna reprimands Arjuna for shirking his righteous duty. He demands the highest work culture. If the karma yoga or the work ethic is destined, it is blended with bhakti yoga or divine devotion. Then the work itself becomes worship or seva yoga. The Lord's advice is relevant here: *Tasmaat sarveshu kaaleshu mamanusmarah yuddha cha*, meaning that under all circumstances remember Him and then fight. Fight here implies performing one's duties.

Making a strong case for the *Gita's* immense relevance in management practices today, Mr. Bhattathiry believes that Western theories on motivation lead to bondage, while theories from the Gita take us to freedom.

Mr Bhattathiry's conclusions are incorrect as he is not a practising Krishna Conscious person. Only Nishkama Karma yoga, that is performing selfless work with results dedicated to Krishna or working on behalf of or for the pleasure of the Supreme Lord, which is the preliminary stage of Bhakti yoga proper, can be called real work culture. If you are working for the Supreme Lord Krishna, only then can you say that work is worship.

It is relevant to mention below some of the world-renowned industrialists and eminent personalities considered experts by business and management schools who have recommended the principles of the *Gita* to be adopted in various management techniques. We do not necessarily agree with their understanding of the *Gita's* teachings nor do we endorse the appropriateness of its application to their methods of management suggested by them. However, the fact that these prominent modern management men have turned to the *Gita* for inspiration is indeed praiseworthy.

A conference paper 'Transformational Leadership from the Bhagavad Gita and the Significance for Human Capital Development' by Muniapan, Balakrishnan and Rajantheran M, presented at the Fourth National Human Resource Management Conference, in Port Dickson, Malaysia, in August 2008 explores this theme. Transformational leadership has received considerable attention in leadership literature during the last two decades. The current business environment requires organizational leaders to be transformational. The transformational leadership style is extremely essential for organizational growth and development as it is the quality of the leaders and their leadership that determines the quality of the organizations. In this paper, the authors explore transformational leadership in the Gita and provide its significance and insights to human capital development.

The scripture provides an inside-out approach to leadership and human capital development. This is self-leadership before leadership. Organizational leaders are advised to first conquer the enemies within, such as desire, anger, greed, arrogance, infatuation, envy, pride or ego, and foolhardiness. It is often said that a leader who conquers the enemies within will conquer his own self as well as others.

The *Gita* was identified as a modern management guide around 30 years ago when perhaps the first such book *Bhagavad Gita: Economic Development and Management* by Avadesh K Srivastava, was published by Abhinav Publications in New Delhi, in 1980. Some other books on the same theme are: *The Gita and the Art of Successful Management* by Ajanta E Chakravarty, published by

HarperCollins, New Delhi, in 2001; *Gita as Management Guide* by Dean Manesh Shrikant of the SP Jain Institute of Management, Mumbai; and *Bhagavad Gita on Effective Leadership: Timeless Wisdom for Leaders* by Pujan Roka, published by Universe (USA) and Jaico (India) in 2008.

Contemporary Leadership Theories

Pujan Roka's *Bhagavad Gita on Effective Leadership* compares the concepts discussed in the *Gita* with contemporary leadership theories and practices and maintains that they are still relevant, effective and applicable to business and organizations today. Leadership is a major trait of top management today. This book indirectly presents major guidelines from the *Gita* to become effective leaders and applies them to modern leadership. Since he works as an executive in a large corporation in the United States, Roka includes scores of examples of outstanding American and global corporate and political leaders and icons. Their achievements and contributions are traced to the guidelines enumerated by the Supreme Lord Krishna in the *Gita*.

The concept of total surrender to the Supreme Lord Krishna is not brought out clearly but the stress on spiritual development to unite with the *Brahaman* (the Supreme Being or the Supreme Consciousness beyond any duality) is mentioned in the initial stages of the book. The author commendably points out that all human beings must move on from their five physical senses to being aware of the mind, moving on to the intellect and finally, to the soul. 'The succession of these states is especially important for an individual who wants to become an effective leader. A leader who focuses on the highest level of consciousness can look at the long-term organizational benefits that span above and beyond his own leadership role and tenure. A leader who has such a focus can achieve benefits that leave a lasting impact on the organization and its shareholders.' One can call it a practical leadership-management master plan.

The Gita in Political Theory

In his book, *World Order: Reflections on the Character of Nations and the Course of History (Penguin India 2014)*, Dr Henry Kissinger refers to the *Gita* and states that the Supreme Lord Krishna considered Arjuna's initial reluctance to fight as wrong because 'life is eternal and cyclical and that the redemption will come through fulfilment of a pre-assigned duty'.

This understanding is inappropriate. The Lord does not recommend in the *Gita* that anyone can just go on a killing spree merely because life is eternal and cyclical. The Lord's enlightening discourse does not aim at such mistaken justification with an intent to promote meaningless massacre just because human life-span on earth is very short and is destined to destruction.

Arjuna's hesitation in the beginning was due to the fact that a strong sense of attachment towards his near relatives suddenly surfaced in his heart when he looked at all those warriors arrayed on both sides of the battlefield. He was sure that almost all of them would die in the war because they were all proud Kshatriyas that would either kill or get killed.

Lord Krishna was certainly aware that Arjuna's conduct at that time was a temporary aberration for he was a trained Kshatriya soldier. The Supreme Lord, no doubt, dwelled at length in His exposition about the distinction between the temporary nature of the physical body and the eternality of the spirit soul, the real living being. He also highlighted the fact that even if Arjuna was incapable of immediate assimilation of this spiritual knowledge, he still had no reason to desist from fighting the war because he was a Kshatriya both by birth and nature. To fight was his duty when an occasion arose.

The Supreme Lord Krishna was gradually elevating Arjuna's understanding and awareness to the point of unconditional surrender because that is the actual duty of the subordinate living entities towards the Supreme God, whether engagement in war or in peace.

Dr Kissinger perhaps infers when he says 'While Lord Krishna's appeal to duty prevails....' that it is the duty based on physical concept of life. No. The Supreme Lord clearly makes the point prominent in the *Gita* that the person's duty should be based on spiritual consciousness. Duty or ***sva dharma*** is of two types. One is based on physical connection and the other on spiritual relationship. The Supreme Lord Krishna lays clear emphasis on the ***sva dharma*** of the living being, the atomic spiritual entity to Himself, the Supreme spiritual entity. This comes out very clearly in His final exhortation in the *Gita* (18/66), He says, 'Surrender unto Me only.' He leaves no scope for ambiguity. No choices. No alternative shelter, not even to the other lesser divine manifestations.

This core message is applicable to all human beings down the ages. Once any person understands this message and surrenders to the Supreme Lord and then carries out his/her worldly duties, then as a spirit soul not identifying with the bodily activities, he/she adopts 'a sakshi bhav' or an attitude of witnessing and leaving the result to the Supreme Lord. Every one of us has to fight his/her personal battle, just as Arjuna did by obeying unconditionally the instructions of the Supreme Lord. When any person is confronted with a formidable choice, the only recourse is to offer the response to the Supreme Lord and also leave its outcome to Him. This is how unconditional surrender has to be applied in real life.

Dr Kissinger has also commented that 'Arjuna, a warrior, has been presented with a war he did not seek'. This again is incorrect. People familiar with the *Mahabharata* are well aware that Arjuna was preparing himself for this very day for thirteen long years during exile collecting arms and weapons from all corners of this universe. He was just waiting to display all his skills and mastery over archery only to finish off his enemies.

Besides Dr Kissinger, many great Sanskrit scholars have also failed in the past. It is extremely difficult to understand the actual import of the *Gita's* teachings unless you have spiritual background and devotion. Mere intellectual brilliance, Sanskrit scholarship or a routine method of comprehension cannot lend one the ability to grasp the esoteric nature of the *Gita's* teachings. They are intelligible only to the initiated. The required qualification for receiving the enlightenment is stated by the Supreme Lord Himself in the *Gita* (4/3). One has to be a friend and devotee of the Lord. Only then the real purport of His discourse will be revealed in the heart of such a devotee. To gain this transcendental knowledge the method proposed in the following verse (4/34) of the *Gita* is:

Tad viddhi pranipatena
Pariprasnena sevaya
Upadeksyanti te jñanam
Jñaninas tattva-darsinah

Just try to learn the truth by approaching a spiritual master. Inquire from him submissively and render service unto him. The self-realized souls can impart knowledge unto you because they have seen the truth.

The Gita for Corporate Motivation

In today's corporate world, a leading Indian newspaper, *The Hindu*, reported on 20 February, 2008: 'The Delhi Metro Rail Corporation does not believe in intense vigilance nor does it rely on hidden cameras to plug leaks and nab wrong-doers. Instead, the organization has turned to the *Bhagavad Gita* to stem corruption, lethargy and negligence. Putting the accent on 'sticking to ethics in the workplace', the organization is attempting to instil the values of honesty, and the moral virtues of hard work and diligence as preached in the *Bhagavad Gita*, which has now emerged as a guidebook for motivating the numbers-driven managers.'

The New Delhi Metro, considered the most modern and efficient in the world, organises yoga lessons for its employees to help them deal with stress and its after-effects. To motivate employees and encourage a positive outlook, quotations from the *Gita* are published in its monthly newsletter and safety bulletins, so that the messages reach everyone from the senior management to the workers and contractors, the Chief Public Relations Officer, Anuj Dayal declared. The Metro's former Managing Director, E Sreedharan, is a fervent believer in the values that the *Bhagavad Gita* preaches. *The Hindu* reports that Metro officials claim that Mr Sreedharan's messages to his employees are peppered with references from the holy book.

Inspiration and Solutions from the Gita

Many of India's captains of business and industry found inspiration and solutions in the Supreme Lord Krishna's advice in the *Gita*. The founder of one of India's largest business and industrial groups, Ghanshyam Das Birla (1893-1983), began his day by reciting verses from the *Bhagavad Gita*. He moved away from his traditional business of money-lending to jute, and founded Birla Jute Mills. It was this understanding that inspired Birla to encourage other Indian businessmen to enter the jute business with him as he went on to expand into other industries. This was the beginning of his vast empire that flourishes in three major Birla groups to this day.

The Indian industrialist, Seth Walchand Hirachand Doshi (1882-1953), who founded an empire in construction, shipping, aircraft and automobiles, was a living example of 'management thoughts' inspired by the *Gita*, which he put into practice. His life was guided by a powerful vision, through which he generated some out-of-the-box strategies. This was accomplished by impeccable planning, unparallelled human resource empowerment and rigorous project management. The founders of these major industrial groups had no management degrees from B-Schools; they received their inspiration from the *Gita*.

Even today, some of India's foremost corporate leaders rely on the *Gita*. An article by Vikas Kumar in *The Economic Times* of 1 June 2007, entitled 'Management by Mantra' mentions a top Indian industrialist, Sanjay Lalbhai of the $500 million Lalbhai Group, and his trust in the *Gita*.

'Through all the ups and downs of his career, Sanjay Lalbhai was guided by the philosophy of *nishkama karma*. When Arvind Mills was teetering on the brink of bankruptcy seven years ago, the managing director could possibly have reached for Robert Andree's *Art of Negotiation* or any of the many other management books lining his office shelves. He was, after all, trying to persuade 23 international banks to restructure over Rs 2000 crore ($40 billion) of debt the company had raised for its new textiles complex in Ahmedabad.

But in his time of crisis, Lalbhai would reach out for an old book he'd read in his youth—the *Bhagavad Gita*. 'I was in an impossible situation and at that point, the ideas of *nishkama karma* really helped me fight the stress and find peace,' he says. 'Good and bad fortune are a matter of time, the *Gita* tells us, and you need to stay driven while detaching yourself from the outcome. It's a philosophy that has guided my work.'

Another top Indian industrialist, Venugopal Dhoot, Chairman of the Videocon Group, a major manufacturer of white goods, spends two hours every day reading the *Gita*. He says 'The *Bhagavad Gita* has taught me the importance of work and how not to get attached to it. It has also helped me to relax and reduce stress levels.'

Management student Kavita Bhardwaj now has her own copy of the *Gita* because she has discovered a new Bible for modern management. And the newest management guru is the Supreme Lord Krishna.

Yet, while trying to assimilate the instructions contained, sometimes doubts may arise and that requires a need to seek clarification to facilitate correct understanding. Therefore, the Lord recommends in the *Gita* (4/34) as to how to go about it:

> *Just try to learn the truth by approaching a spiritual master. Inquire from him submissively and render service unto him. The self-realized souls can impart knowledge unto you because they have seen the truth.*

Appendix: Karma Capitalism

How is this Karma Capitalism from the Gita practical for today's corporate world?

Karma Capitalism is not a concept from the *Gita* at all. Such fancy concepts and phases are periodically coined and promoted by pseudo-intellectuals and market strategists of business schools and management institutes. Such whimsical theories and concepts are differently defined by different management gurus. Moreover, karma as defined in the *Gita* has nothing to do with either capitalism or communism.

First, the entire world has to accept one God and that God to be a person, not an abstract impersonal entity. Second, that God is the Supreme Lord Krishna. This must be accepted unconditionally. This is a prerequisite. Only then the *Bhagavat Gita* and its teachings can have any relevance to an individual, a corporation, a country or the whole world.

Next, the Supreme Lord Krishna has assertively declared in the *Gita* (4/13) that He has created four classes of human society and these classes have been allotted karma (work) according to their inherited nature (18/42, 43, 44) and not on the basis of birth. The *Gita* does not support the present distorted version of the caste system existing in India.

The Law of Karma or theory of karma is one of the basic principles of Vedic philosophy. This is accurately explained in the *Vedanta* and other Vedic literature. The *Gita* offers concise clarifications on this topic. The Supreme Lord Krishna speaks in the *Gita* (3/27) about the living entities perform actions due to influence of three modes of His material energy (***prakriti***) namely, ***Satva*** – goodness, ***Rajah*** – passion and ***Tamah***—ignorance. The Supreme Lord Krishna further highlights in the *Gita* (18/40) that there is no person existing either here or among the demi-gods in the higher planetary systems who is free from these modes of material energy.

The Lord also informs Arjuna during the discourse of the *Gita* (14/18) that as a matter of reaction after death, karma in the mode of goodness promotes one to heavenly planets and that in the mode of passion brings back the performer to the planet earth. Karma performed in the abominable mode of ignorance obliges the performer to go to the hellish planets below the earth.

Hence, the conclusive advice by the Supreme Lord in the *Gita* (3/9) is to act on His behalf exclusively for His pleasure, otherwise karma performed piously or impiously will only perpetuate the living entity's conditioned existence within this universe to enjoy or suffer karmic reactions. This advice is because the *Gita* aims at spiritual liberation and not to rot in the corridor of Maya in this world.

In today's materialistic civilization, when an attempt is made to develop a classless society, how can the corporate world find any scope for implementing the karma principles of the *Gita* based on the Vedic class system?

Karma capitalism promotes consciousness but how can it promote Krishna Consciousness?

The Karma Consciousness basically teaches that the plain-old profit centre should be transformed as karmic profit centre. This transformation is aimed at building positive karmic effect that one offers something gratuitously with the knowledge that, down the road, she/he will be repaid many times over. The promotion of such consciousness is useless because positive karma also perpetuates the person's bondage here which is not the ultimate aim of the *Gita's* teachings.

In the *Gita* (12/11) the Supreme Lord gives a hint about how one's karma can gradually elevate a person to Krishna consciousness. For a starter, one can donate to social welfare institutions. By such acts of giving the fruits of one's work, the person's mind becomes purified. She/he is then able to understand Krishna consciousness. This process is technically called ***karmarpanam***.

How will this be translated in modern business practices?

a. Employers as well as employees need to be selfless, respectful, kind and compassionate.

b. The enterprises must set aside substantial portion of profit for the purposes of social welfare after providing for expansion and diversification.

c. They can render financial assistance in times of natural calamities like earthquake, flood and famine, proactively instead of waiting for government's response.

d. They can support rural medical supply and mid-day meal schemes for school children.

e. Construction of schools, hospitals and other public amenities can be undertaken.

f. They will not produce and sell shoddy goods as quality goods: they will not destroy natural resources to make short-term profits: they will not prepare false accounts or similar unethical practices like paying bribes to get approvals or contacts. They will follow all the legal requirements in manufacturing, marketing, distribution, staff and public relations, in fact, in managing the company and charge a fair price that provides value for money.

In other words, the enterprises must incorporate social responsibility as well as ethical methods in their practices.

On top of all, the business houses must help in whatever way they can genuine Krishna conscious preachers in their work to spread the *Gita's* message because it promotes a non-sectarian universal religion.

How can it be applied according to the specific teachings of Lord Krishna?

While enlightening Arjuna systematically in the eleventh chapter of the *Gita*, the Supreme Lord outlines the process of surrender in a progressive manner in the twelfth chapter verses number 8, 9, 10 and 11, as stated below:

Just fix your mind upon Me, the Supreme Lord, and engage all your intelligence in Me. Thus you will live in Me always, without a doubt.
My dear Arjuna, O winner of wealth, if you cannot fix your mind upon Me without deviation, then follow the regulative principles

of Bhakti-yoga. In this way develop a desire to attain Me. If you cannot practise the regulations of Bhakti-yoga, then just try to work for Me, because by working for Me you will come to the perfect stage.

If, however, you are unable to work in this consciousness of Me, then try to act giving up all results of your work and try to be self-situated.

Karma means both causality as well as result of actions. As a matter of chain reactions, since many past lives, we have become addicted to perform actions with a desire to enjoy results. This can be broken down. But this is not possible overnight. There are two techinal words: ***Krtritva*** and ***Bhogtritva***. Kritritva is action and Bhogtritva is enjoyment. Therefore, the Supreme Lord advises us to give up Bhogtritva, that is, enjoyment of the five senses and keep performing actions, that is, Kritritva, to offer the results to the Supreme Lord. Hence, you can continue to perform action and start surrendering results to the Supreme Lord which is known as ***Krishna karmarpanam***. By this act, gradual purification of consciousness will take place. This, in turn, will result in total surrender over a period.

Although Arjuna was a warrior involved in material actions like any other modern man in today's world, he was leading a life based on the regulative principles of the ***Varna-Ashrama*** (socio-religious) system existing then. He, therefore, had a pure mind which enabled him to grasp what the Supreme Lord wanted him to do ultimately.

How are Indian gurus and university professors cashing on this concept without understanding it fully?

The persons claiming to represent Buddhism and Jainism declare there is nothing like God and ultimately everything is zero. Their philosophy is known as ***Shunyavada*** or Voidism. The followers of the philosophy of Adi Shankaracharya believe that the ultimate reality is abstract ***Brahman*** which is a formless entity. Their philosophy is known as ***Advaitavada*** or monism.

Thus, for 14 centuries, from 300 BC to 1100 AD, India was mostly influenced by voidists and monists. This means most of the population was atheistic. A lack of a true spiritual awareness and indifference towards philosophical research made the masses accept their deliberate misinterpretation of Vedic teachings. These voidists and monists were seen as religious saints and scholars then.

Although ***Bhakti Yoga***, or devotional service to God Krishna/ Vishnu, was revived with great vigour in the latter centuries by the advent of Shripad Ramanujacharya and Shripad Madhvacharya, many of the modern-day Indian gurus and university professors, prefer to thrive on the Adi Sankaracharya's misinterpreted version of the *Gita* and the *Vedanta*. Hence, the so-called gurus and thinkers of Indian society enthusiastically support and promote such concepts as Karma Capitalism, without understanding what they are talking about.

I. Meera Sanyal lays emphasis on building good employer-employee relationships while speaking on Karma Capitalism.

II. Sisodia claims that Karma Capitalism happens when companies work for the benefit of all stakeholders.

III. Gautum Jain says that success is achieved through the three disciplines of concentration, consistency and cooperation while peace is gained by cessation of agitations through control and direction of one's desires. He adds that the *Vedanta* provides a clear means to attain these two ends.

He does not quote the Supreme Lord Krishna's statement on this. The peace formula is suggested by the Lord in the *Gita* (2/66) as under:

> One who is not connected with the Supreme
> (in Krishna Consciousness) can have neither
> transcendental intelligence nor a steady mind,
> without which there is no possibility of peace.
> And how can there be any happiness without peace?

IV. Both Gautum Jain and Kumar Rao agree that they constantly come across sceptics (according to them, but actually the wise ones), who find it difficult to accept that the ancient theories can be applied in the modern world.

V. C.K. Prahlad says, 'It is the idea that corporations can simultaneously create value and social justice.' He calls this 'Inclusive Capitalism' instead of Karma Capitalism.

VI. The eighty-year-old Shrila Partha Sarathy, an enthusiastic proponent of the impersonal view of the Vedanta, says, 'You can't succeed in business unless you develop the intellect, which controls the mind and the body.'

VII. An ardent advocate of the Vedanta, Kumar Rao says that the main objective 'is to help you to discover your purpose in life'. He does not speak about that.
The purpose is stated by the Supreme Lord Krishna in the *Gita* (15/15):

I am seated in everyone's heart, and from Me
come remembrance, knowledge and forgetfulness.
By all the Vedas, I am to be known. Indeed, I am
the compiler of Vedanta and I am knower of the Vedas.

From the above, it is clear that none of the Indian gurus or the professors highlight the most important factor: the Supreme Lord Krishna. The Lord Himself clearly articulates in the *Gita* (18/14) that He is one of the factors with which any karma or action is accomplished as under:

> *The place of action (the body), the performer,*
> *the various senses, the many different kinds of*
> *endeavour, and ultimately the Supersoul –*
> *these are five factors of action.*

We must understand that the Supreme Lord Krishna is the speaker, the subject-matter and the goal of the *Gita*. All living beings have an eternal relationship with Him. The revival of this connection with Him is the only purpose of human life. Today a white collar or a blue collar worker can succeed by following the method outlined in verses 8, 9, 10 and 11 of the chapter 12 of the *Gita*. Without recognizing the supremacy of Lord Krishna and His all-pervasive presence in each atom, proton and neutron, simply a paradigm shift in business dealings in the name of Karma Capitalism cannot benefit anyone in the ultimate sense.

What are the five core principles of Karma Capitalism with Krishna Consciousness?

A cursory glance reveals that most business gurus recommend the following in the name of Karma Capitalism.

a. Corporate Social Responsibility.

b. Doing well by doing good.

c. Concentration, consistency and cooperation.

d. Purpose of life.

e. Corporate philanthropy.

f. Protecting the environment, contributing to community and improving workers' lives.

g. A shift from a production orientation to a customer focus.

h. Improved customer relationship and increased employee loyalty.

i. Relationship marketing.

j. Higher wages, better quality products.

k. Work for the benefit of all the stakeholders instead of only shareholders.

The above principles constitute fundamental business ethics and norms of almost all commercial dealings. Since deviation from these had affected both the Enterprises and the Entrepreneurs, out of a guilty conscience, they are now contemplating to reincorporate these principles in the name of Karma Capitalism which may do good only for increased business activities and profits but nothing else.

The present situation is that both employers and employees from top to bottom are operating from the platform of animal consciousness. Unless they rise to human consciousness, the desired change in the template of business dealings or a paradigm shift in general cannot be brought about. It requires a proper mindset on the parts of both of them.

The five core principles of Karma Capitalism with Krishna Consciousness are:

1. Krishna the God is the Supreme controller.
2. It is difficult to realize God is a person and that there exists eternally a spiritual world full of bliss. It is required to develop a purified consciousness to realise this. For this, one must be free from four major sins: consuming intoxicants, eating meat, gambling and illicit sex for carnal enjoyment.
3. Lust, greed and envy are the causes of all sins. These can be gradually subdued and finally eliminated completely, only by chanting the holy names of Krishna in the form of Mahamantra: Hare Krishna Hare Krishna Krishna Krishna Hare Hare Hare, Rama Hare Rama Rama Rama Hare Hare. There are no conditions for chanting this mantra. A top boss can chant in his air-conditioned cabin during lunch time. A factory worker can do so in his Tool Room. One can achieve peace of mind only by this process.
4. All should at least accept in theory that the real living being is a spirit soul and not the body. She/he is eternally related to the Supreme Lord Krishna, the Supreme Spirit Soul. It is a master and servant relationship. The servant's duty is to spread the message of his master. If one cannot directly engage fully, then she/he should give in charity to a genuine Krishna Conscious preacher 10 per cent of annual gross income to help in promoting Krishna Consciousness.
5. One must study the *Bhagavat Gita* with commentary by a bona fide Vaishnava Acharya to get the correct understanding of what the Supreme Lord originally spoke to Arjuna and through him to the whole world.

Chapter 9

Harish, Harry, Hurry, Hari

After obtaining a Masters degree in Electronics Engineering and a post-graduate degree in Business Management, Harish Gupta landed a highly paid job in the USA. Arriving in Chicago, he was called 'Harry' by his colleagues. With rapid promotions in a few years, he had a luxurious home, a vacation condo in Florida and a flat in Mumbai. As the Vice-President of his company, he became the president of his professional association and a host of friends and colleagues respected and admired him for his success.

But Harry had to pay the price for all this so-called success. The constant 'hurry, hurry' took its toll. The never-ending working hours at the office took him away from his wife and two children as he hardly spent any time with them. The tension and the stress of holding his job and meeting the almost impossible targets resulted in unending tension, stress, high blood pressure and, finally, a heart attack. His wife threatened divorce and moving to Mumbai. Every morning, he swallows a handful of pills to keep his health problems under control; and every night, a couple of sedatives to go to sleep.

Is there any way out for him from this mess? Can he regain his balance in life? Is it possible to work as a high-powered executive and also keep his body and mind in good shape? The answer is to surrender to Hari. Hari? Yes, 'Hari'...for this is one of the most beautiful names for the Supreme Lord Krishna. The word 'Hari' means a thief and the Supreme Lord Krishna is given this name because He steals the hearts of His devotees. So Harry, surrender to Hari – the Supreme Lord Krishna. "How can I surrender to the Supreme Lord Krishna? After all, I am not illiterate... what with my qualifications and a senior position in my company. I control and direct hundreds of employees, manage millions of dollars for the company so I have the brains to think to manage my own life instead of letting Krishna take over," protests Harry.

Harry has problems but he will not surrender. So did Arjuna on the battle field of Kuruskhetra. Although Arjuna was cheated out of his kingdom, and spent thirteen long years in exile in the forest and was still not given his due, he was unwilling to fight his cousins. The Supreme Lord Krishna urges him to fight his evil cousins but he is hesitant. Today, it's the education, training and ego that stops Harry from surrendering to the Supreme Lord Krishna. He is not the only one, most so-called educated and successful persons do not surrender either. This initial reaction has been the same down the ages.

Greatest Scholar of His Age

It is stated in the epic Mahabharata that the Supreme Lord Krishna was transferred at birth from Kamsa's prison in Mathura to the home of Nanda Maharaja in Gokula. In the Shrimad Bhagavatam (10/8/13) the sage Garga Muni, the Priest of Yadava Clan, revealed during the name, giving ceremony of Krishna as follows:

Your son appears as an incarnation in every yuga (millennium). In the past He assumed three different colours – white (in Satya Yuga), Red (in Treta Yuga),
Yellow (in Kali Yuga) - and now (Dwarapara Yuga) He has appeared in Blackish colour.

This reference to "Yellow" colour pertaining to Kali Yuga confirms the appearance of the Supreme Lord Krishna as Chaitanya Mahaprabhu because His body was of Golden (yellow) complexion. Therefore, on the authority of the Bhagavat Mahapurana, the Gaudiya Vaishnavas believe and accept Chaitanya Mahaprabhu is the Supreme Lord Krishna Himself appeared to teach the people of this degraded age by His own example how to surrender and to experience the ecstatic love of God.

Those who are not willing to accept this scriptural evidence, can still consider the historical facts about Shri Chaitanya Mahaprabhu which is there for everyone to see.

Shri Chaitanya Mahaprabhu (1486 -1534) was born in the 16th Century in Mayapur, in the district of Nadia in West Bengal. When he was eight years old, he started to learn from a reputed scholar, Gangadasa, a resident of the same village . In just two years, he had acquired a grasp of Sanskrit grammar and rhetoric. He went on reading many more classics. In two years, at the age of ten, he became a scholar in Sanskrit grammar, the *shruti* (the *Vedas*), the *smrti* (the Ramayana, the Mahabharata, the Eighteen Puranas and other scriptures passed orally down the generations) and *nyaya* (the ancient system of logic).

Just then, his elder brother Vishwarupa became a sannyasi and left home. Soon after, his father died; he consoled his mother. At the age of 15, he got married in the same village. At this time, at his age, he was considered the top scholar of Nadia, the renowned seat of *nyaya* philosophy and Sanskrit learning. Nadia was famous as the village of learned pundits and such was the high reputation of Chaitanya's scholarship that no one in this village was ready to challenge him in a debate. Many pundits came to challenge him and became his students after being defeated by him. A very famous Sanskrit scholar, Keshav Kashmiri, came all the way from Kashmir to challenge him and also lost, such was his grasp on scriptures and logic.

At the peak of his intellectual fame came his turning point when his father died. He had to go to the holy pilgrimage Gaya to perform rituals for liberating his forefathers. On that occasion he met a renowned saint by the name Ishwara Puri of Madhwa Sampradaya and requested him for guidance in spirituality. He was then initiated in chanting Hare Krishna Maha Mantra by him. As he recited it, he was transformed and he cast aside all his knowledge and became a committed devotee of the Supreme Lord Krishna. So full of his devotion, he could not hold himself from singing the great mantra of 'Hare Krishna Hare Krishna Krishna Krishna Hare Hare, Hare Rama Hare Rama Rama Rama Hare Hare' and started dancing in the streets and roads, while his followers were playing the drums and cymbals. His constant refrain was 'Haribol, Haribol' or recite the name of Hari. He became perhaps the greatest example of Bhagkti Yoga (loving devotion to the Supreme Lord Krishna based on the philosophy of the Bhagavata Maha Purana and the Bhagavad Gita). So, if the most famous scholar of his time, Chaitainya, renounced all his learning and surrendered to the Supreme Lord Krishna, why not Harry or Harish?

Outstanding Example of Surrender

More recently, His Divine Grace Bhaktivedanta Shrila Prabhupada, the founder of Hare Krishna movement all over the world, is another outstanding example of surrendering to the Supreme Lord Krishna.

Born Abhay Charan De in 1896 in a humble house in Calcutta (now Kolkata), he went to the prestigious Scottish Churches College and got a western education. He graduated in 1920 with majors in English, philosophy and economics. After getting married, he managed a small pharmaceutical business and supported his wife and children.

In 1922, when Abhay Babu first met, Bhaktisiddhanta Saraswati Thakura Prapupad, the latter said that as an English-speaking young Babu, he should spread the message of Chaitanya Mahaprabhu in the English-speaking world. Abhay Babu argued by saying that as nobody would listen to our message as India was not an independent country. Bhaktisiddhanta Saraswati replied that the message of Chaitanya Mahaprabhu did not depend on who is ruling the country. It can be spread in any place, at any time and under any circumstances. This reply made him surrender to Bhaktisiddhanta Saraswati in his heart, accepting him as his spiritual master. Later in 1933, Abhay Babu was formally initiated as his disciple. In 1944, he started publishing a magazine in English, *Back to Godhead*, from his home. Such was his surrender that he acted as the designer, publisher, editor, copy editor and distributor.

From 1950 onwards, Abhay Babu lived frugally at the medieval Radha-Damodar Mandir in Vrindavan where he started to translate the scripture Bhagavat Maha Purana. In September 1959, Abhay Babu, always dressed in white, became Shrila Prabhupada, now dressed in saffron. To spread the message of Chaitanya Mahaprabhu around the world, he left India in 1965, obtaining free passage on a freight ship called the *Jaladuta*. He had a suitcase, an umbrella, several boxes of the Shrimad Bhagavatam translated by him in English and just eight US dollars. On his arrival in September in Boston, he stayed with Gopal Agarwal at Butler, Pennsylvania. Then he moved to New York in a storefront at 26, Second Avenue. Determined to spread the message of the Supreme Lord Krishna, he went to the nearby Tompkins Square park and started to sing "Hare Krishna" mantra by himself. Some curious people gathered around him and later joined him. Soon, this became a daily routine and then devotion for all of them. When more and more followers were attracted to him he founded the International Society for Krishna Consciousness (ISKCON) in July 1966. He subsequently became popular as Prabhupada.

During the twelve years from his arrival in Boston, until he left his body in 1977, he circled the globe 14 times to six continents; established more than 108 temples across the globe with many other institutions; founded Bhativedanta Book Trust, the largest publisher of ancient Vaishnava religious texts; authored more than 80 books on Vedantic philosophy; introduced annual celebrations like the processions of Jagannath Chariot festival in many cities of the world; continued to direct the publication of *Back to Godhead* to become a global magazine of his movement, among other notable achievements.

The Beatle Who Loved the Sweet Lord

George Harrison, the guitarist, singer and songwriter of perhaps the most famous pop group, The Beatles, had it all - money and fame beyond the dreams of most people. Yet he felt a deep emptiness within him that urged him to explore Indian spirituality.

During the shooting of the film *Help!*, on location in the Bahamas in 1965, a Hindu devotee presented each Beatle with a book about reincarnation. Harrison's interest in Indian culture and in Hinduism was awakened. During a visit to India the next year, Harrison learnt to play the sitar and visited several Hindu holy places and met many gurus. In 1968, he travelled to India with the other Beatles to participate in meditation with Maharishi Mahesh Yogi. In the summer of 1969, he produced the single *Hare Krishna*

Mantra, performed by the devotees of the London Radha Krishna Temple. His quest ended when he met Shrila Prabhupada and started chanting the Hare Krishna maha-mantra. He and fellow Beatle John Lennon met Shrila Prabhupada and he surrendered to the Supreme Lord Krishna by becoming a life-long devotee until his death in 2001. He gave away his mansion, Letchmore Heath, in the north of London, to ISKCON and it was renamed as Bhagktivedanta Manor.

"Everybody is looking for Krishna," he said, "Some don't realise that they are, but they are..." His devotion became prominent in his work. After this turning point in his life, Harrison's albums - *The Hare Krishna Mantra, My Sweet Lord, All Things Must Pass, Living in the Material World,* and *Chants of India* - are greatly influenced by Krishna consciousness. In October 1970, *My Sweet Lord* from his UK Number One hit triple album *All Things Must Pass* is primarily about the Supreme Lord Krishna. When released as a single, *My Sweet Lord* topped the charts on both sides of the Atlantic in 1971. Among the 500 Greatest Songs of All Time by *Rolling Stone* magazine, it is ranked 454. *Living in the Material World* ends with the words: "Got to get out of this place by the Lord Sri Krishna's grace, my salvation from the material world." The song *That Which I Have Lost* from the album *Somewhere in England* is directly inspired by the Gita. In his devotional music, Harrison drew millions closer to spirituality and felt so empowered by his devotion that he said, "Chanting Hare Krishna makes me feel invincible."

From Billionaire to Bhakta

Alfred Ford, the great-grandson of the famous Henry Ford who gave the world the car named after him and the system of assembly line mass production, is another living example of surrender to the Supreme Lord Krishna. "Though I belonged to a family which had everything, still, there was unhappiness and frustration," he said in an interview with *The Times of India*. "I wasn't satisfied with material opulence. I was looking for reality that was eternal. I wanted to know what God looked like. I was looking for a personal connection with God, a relationship with him." His life defining moment was when he bought a music album of George Harrison when he was in college. As he listened to the first *bhajan* or devotional song he found himself crying. "It touched something very, very deep in my heart. It was a very profound experience. I realised it was the concept of God I was looking for – Govinda, the most attractive, the protector of cows, the most beautiful, always youthful, eyes like blossoming flowers..."

"I read Prabhupada's translation of the Gita, and soon, I started to change my lifestyle. I had turned vegetarian in college and I had stopped drinking, and then I started cooking vegetarian food and offering it to Krishna as *prasadam*. I started chanting on my *japa mala* (chanting beads) and studying Prabhupada's books, he went on. Soon a guru-disciple relationship began to develop between the 20-something heir to one of America's biggest fortunes and the 80-something founder of Hinduism's biggest spiritual movements of modern times. Finally, they met. "I was very nervous as I knew this was a great personality. So I bowed to him and as I was coming up, he said, "So you are Henry Ford's great- grandson. Where is he now?' And that question made me realise that life is so temporary." He surrendered and became a devotee.

As a devotee, he rises early at 4 a. m. to start his chanting and worships until 9 a. m. Then he gets down to his office work as a Trustee of the Ford Motor Company Fund taking care of its charitable work, manages an IT company and other investments. "All this is pure business," he says, "Krishna's message to Arjuna was not to give up his position as a warrior and go to meditate in the woods, but to fulfil the purpose here in this material world. Go ahead and achieve what you have to, be the best of what you can be, but at the same time, don't forget your spiritual life. Wealth is a gift from God. It's best if it is used to serve Him ultimately."

Is Surrender the Answer?

All this was accomplished by these devotees solely through total surrender to the Supreme Lord Krishna. If with surrender to the Supreme Lord Krishna, just one person can become the mode of the Supreme Lord to establish so many mammoth religious institutions, find peace in one's music, balance one's business with *bhakti*, then Harish or Harry can also attain balance and peace in his life while making progress in this world.

Why surrender to Lord Krishna?

Firstly, the Lord clearly says in the Gita that He is the Supreme Controller of this universe. In this universe, there are fourteen planetary systems and there are many rulers controlling the functions of each planet called *Ishwaras*, But the Supreme Lord Krishna is the controller of all these planetary rulers. He is the *Adhyaksha*, the Superintendent, under whose supervision the creation, maintenance, and annihilation of this entire cosmos goes on and on. He is the origin of all existences, the ultimate cause of all causes.

> *O conqueror of Wealth, there is no truth superior to Me. Everything rests upon Me, as pearls are strung on a thread. (7/ 7)*
>
> *This material nature, which is one of My energies, is working under My direction, O son of Kunti, producing all moving and*

non-moving beings. Under its rule this manifestation is created and annihilated again and again. (9/10)

I am the source of all spiritual and material worlds. Everything emanates from Me. The wise who know this perfectly engage in My devotional service and worship Me with all their hearts. (10/8)

These pronouncements of the Supreme Lord Krishna have been sometines misinterpreted. Some commentators have failed to understand them. The Supreme Lord proved them wrong beyond all doubt by revealing his '*virat roop*' or 'universal form' in which the entire universe is contained within Him. Thus, Arjuna's doubts were all dispelled. The Supreme Lord informs Arjuna that placing Himself as a Super-Soul inside the heart of every living being, He closely supervises their functions, desires and the thought process. He announces:

Yet in this body there is another, a transcendental enjoyer, who is the Lord, the supreme proprietor, who exists as the overseer and approver, and who is known as the Super soul (13/23)

He further declares that He personally enters into each planet to control all activities:

I enter into each planet, and by My energy they stay in orbit. I become the moon and thereby supply the juice of life to all vegetables. (15/13)

The Lord clarifies that we cannot even digest the food we eat without His effective monitoring:

I am the fire of digestion in every living body, and I am the air of life, outgoing and incoming, by which I digest the four kinds of foodstuff. (15/14)

What's more, the Lord is always directing all our mental and intellectual functions. Our ability to understand and remember comes from Him. We cannot even forget without His approval. This is the undeniable truth. He clarifies:

I am seated every one's heart, and from Me come remembrance, knowledge and forgetfulness. By all the Vedas, I am to be known.
Indeed, I am the compiler of Vedanta, and I am the knower of the Vedas. (15/15)

The Supreme Lord is situated as *Paramatma* (super soul) in everyone's heart, and it is from Him that all our activities are initiated. Every living person forgets everything of his past life, but has to act according to the direction of the Supreme Lord, who is a silent witness to all his activities. Therefore, a living person works according to his *karma* or past deeds. The Supreme Lord Krishna gives him whatever knowledge he requires , releases whatever he needs to remember, and takes away whatever he needs to forget.

The Supreme Lord is situated in everyone's heart,
O Arjuna, and is directing the wanderings of all living entities, who are seated as on a machine, made of the material energy. (18/61)

During the cycle of life and death, the soul changes many physical bodies even in human form. After changing bodies, the living person forgets his past deeds, but the Super Soul, as the knower of the past, present and future, remains the witness of all his activities. Therefore, all activities of living persons are directed by this Super Soul. The living person gets what he deserves and is carried by the physical body. This physical body is created in the material energy under the direction of the Super Soul. As soon as a living person is placed in a particular type of body, he has to work under the confines of that physical boundary. A person seated in a speeding motorcar goes faster than one in slower car, though the living persons or the drivers, may be the same. Similarly, by the order of Supreme Soul, physical nature fashions a particular type of body to a particular type of living person, so that he may work according to his past desires.

There are many professed atheists who deny and defy the very existence of God since time immemorial. Yet, they also exist within the control of the Lord. He explicitly expresses what He does with them:

> *They say that this world is unreal, that there is no foundation and that there is no God in control. It is produced of sex desire, and has no cause other than lust. (16/18)*

> *Those who are envious and mischievous, who are the lowest among men, are cast by Me into the ocean of material existence, into various demoniac species of life. (16/19)*

> *Attaining repeated birth amongst the species of demoniac life, such persons can never approach Me. Gradually they sink down to the most abominable type of existence. (16/20)*

Following assertion of the Supreme Lord Hari amply corroborates the age old proverb of the Indian masses that not a blade of grass moves without His sanction:

O mighty-armed Arjuna, according to the Vedanta there are five causes for the accomplishment of all action. Now learn of these from Me. (18/13)

The place of action (the body), the performer, the various senses, the many different kinds of endevour, and ultimately the Super-soul – these are the five factors of action. (18/14)

The Supreme Lord is situated in everyone's heart, O Arjuna, and is directing the wanderings of all living entities, who are seated as on a machine, made of the material energy. (18/61)

Finally, the Supreme Lord Krishna is known as *Hrishikesha. Hrishika* means senses and *isha* means controller. This means that the Supreme Lord controls and guides all our five sensory functions and the activities of His devotees directly while others are controlled through the agency of His *Maya*, the material nature. Whether theists or atheists, nobody is outside His control.

Actual Identity of a Living Being

When the Supreme Lord Krishna observed that the initially enthusiastic Arjuna was unwilling to fight on reaching the battlefield of Kurukshetra, He realised that this would jeopardise His objective of annihilating the evil kings present there. So He persuaded in different ways Arjuna to get up and fight. At the outset, the Lord imparted to Arjuna of the actual identity of a living being as a spirit soul and not body:

For the soul there is never birth nor death. Nor, having once been, does he ever cease to be. He is unborn, eternal, ever

-existing, undying and primeval. He is not slain when the body is slain.

O Partha, how can a person who knows that the soul is indestructible, unborn, eternal and immutable, kill anyone or cause anyone to kill?

As a person puts on new garments, giving up old ones, similarly, the soul accepts new material bodies, giving up the old and useless ones.

(*Bhagavat Gita*, Chapter 2, Texts 20, 21 & 22)

Even from the physical concept of life, the Lord argued, Arjuna should not desist from fighting:

Considering your specific duty as a khsatriya, you should know that there is no better engagement for you than fighting on religious principles; and so there is no need for hesitation.

O Partha, happy are the kshatriyas to whom such fighting opportunities come unsought, opening for them the doors of the heavenly planets.

(*Bhagavat Gita*, Ch 2, Texts 31 & 32)

O son of Kunti, either you will be killed on the battlefield and attain the heavenly planets, or you will conquer and enjoy the earthly kingdom. Therefore, get up and fight with determination.

(*Bhagavat Gita*, Ch 2, Text 37)

If you do not act according to My direction and do not fight, then you will be falsely directed. By your nature, you will have to be engaged in warfare.

Under illusion you are now declining to act according to My direction, But, compelled by your own nature, you will act all the same, O son of Kunti.

(*Bhagavat Gita*, Ch 18, Texts 59 & 60)

In this way, the Supreme Lord promoted His objectives and succeeded when Arjuna finally responded positively to the Supreme Lord's inspired discourse. Arjuna was convinced and fell at the feet of the Lord saying:

My dear Krishna, O infallible One, my illusion is now gone. I have regained my memory by Your mercy, and I am now firm and free from doubt and am prepared to act according to Your instructions.

(*Bhagavat Gita*, Ch 18, Text 73)

Thus Arjuna surrendered totally to the Supreme Lord and fought the battle as the Supreme Lord guided him to victory. But for Harry, the Supreme Lord shows him the path of 'Nishkama karma yoga' for it is for those whose minds are impure with innumerable worldly desires.

So while working as a senior executive, engaged in his daily and demanding work, Harry surrenders to the Supreme Lord Krishna. Now he has two clear paths to start regaining his inner balance: nishkama karma yoga when he does not work for a reward but offers it all to the Supreme Lord Krishna. So he does not have any tension nor worry about the results or outcome as he is working for the Supreme Lord and all his rewards are for the Supreme Lord.

Or, he can follow dhyana yoga when he can sit silently and meditate upon the impersonal and un-manifest Brahman. . As admitted by the Supreme Lord Himself in the Gita (12/5), this is a more difficult path to follow in the humdrum of his lifestyle that is action oriented. But some persons do follow this path as well. Moreover, this process only leads to partial realisation of the Supreme. Ultimately, both the paths of karma yoga and dhyan yoga inevitably lead to the final stage of bhakti yoga - the loving service to Hari who has won his heart.

But how does he start? Simple, start chanting the Mahamantra:

Hare Krishna Hare Krishna,
Krishna Krishna Hare Hare,
Hare Rama Hare Rama,
Rama Rama Hare Hare.

Sit silently in the early morning or in the evening and start chanting this mantra loud and clear for at least half an hour. Use cymbals to provide you the pattern of its rhythm. How does it work? Once you start chanting, you get into its rhythm, and it echoes inside your brain. Since your skull is shaped like a sphere, the positive vibrations reverberate inside. Gradually, your adverse thoughts begin to evaporate and your mind becomes clear. As time goes by, and you keep chanting daily, this effect gathers momentum and you get into a stage of ecstasy with the Supreme Lord Krishna as your beloved. If you chant in the morning, the positive effect lasts the whole day and you go about your work with a detached smile. No tension, no stress. Harish's wife joined him from day one and soon his children also joined. In a few months, the Mahamantra transforms their lives. Harish does not need medicines or alcohol to keep going. His performance improved at work. He has regained his balance. After his surrender, he has come full circle from Harish to Harry to hurry and finally to Hari.

Notes and References

General

1. The references from the Ramayana, Mahabharata and the Bhagavad Gita are from the personal knowledge of the author who has studied them extensively.
2. Bhagavat Gita – The English translations for the Sanskrit slokas are from *Bhagavat Gita As It Is* by A.C Bhaktivedanta Shrila Prabhupad.
3. Bhagavatam – The English translations of the Sanskrit slokas *Shrimad Bhagavatam* by A.C Bhaktivedanta Shrila Prabhupad has been used.
4. Global Financial Meltdown 2008 – The causes and case studies for this event were researched on the Internet, especially Wikipedia.

Chapter 01

A. The number of warriors in a '*kshoni*' has been obtained from *Mahabharata by Shriji Dasa, Published by Rasbihari Lal &*

Sons, Lio Bazaar, Vrindaban - 281121, UP.

B. Warren Buffet and Bill Gates - Information from the media and Internet.

C. Immanuel Kant - Page 161 of *The Ideas of Immanuel Kant* by Bertrand Schulman, New Jersey: Philosophical Publishing, 1984.

Chapter 02

A. C. Bhaktivedanta Shrila Prabhupad biography source — Shrila Prabhupada Lilamritam by His Holiness Sat Swarup Maharaj.

Chapter 03

A. Global Financial Meltdown 2008 for US and Indian companies—Information from the media and Internet.

B. Management qualities — From basic management texts and author's personal experience in the corporate sector.

Chapter 04

A. Major Departments of a Company or Corporation — From basic management texts, Internet and author's personal experience in the corporate sector.

Chapter 05

A. Modern Management Concepts and Techiques — From management texts and Internet.

B. Marketing Management — Author's personal experience in the corporate sector.

Chapter 06

A. The two examples used are from real life but their names have been changed to preserve their privacy.

B. Managing and surviving recession — Information on the 2008 financial meltdown from the media and Internet.

Chapter 07

A. This chapter is based on two articles written by the author for the GVA Magazine, *Bhagavat Vani.*

Chapter 08

A. BusinesWeek of 30 October 2006.

B. Charles Chow Hoi - **www.emeraldinsight.com**

C. Balakrishnan Muniapan - Managerial Effectiveness from the Perspectives of the Bhagavad Gita' was presented at the School of Business, Curtin University of Technology, Sarawak, Malaysia.

D. M.P. Bhattathiry, *Bhagavad Gita And Managerial Effectiveness http://www.boloji.com/hinduism/073.htm*

E. Muniapan, Balakrishnan and Rajantheran M. —*'Transformational leadership from the Bhagavad Gita and the significance for human capital development'*

F. ***'The Gita and the Art of Successful Management'*** by Ajanta E. Chakravarty published by HarperCollins, New Delhi in 2001;

G. ***Gita as Management Guide*** Dean Manesh Shrikant of SP Jain Institute of Management, Mumbai

H. *Bhagavad Gita on Effective Leadership: Timeless Wisdom for Leaders* by Pujan Roka published by iUniverse (USA) and Jaico (India) in 2008.

I. Mahatma Gandhi — Collected Works.

J. Delhi Metro — *The Hindu* news report.

K. G. D. Birla — Internet.

L. Seth Walchand Hirachand Doshi - Internet.

M. Sanjay Lalbhai of Arvind Group and Venugopal Dhoot chairman of Videocon group — 'Management by Mantra' by Vikas Kumar in *The Economic Times* , 1 June 2007.

Chapter 09

A. The example used is from real life but the name has been changed to preserve his privacy.

B. Chaitanya Mahaprabhu — Information from the Internet.

C. George Harrison – Internet.

D. Alfred Ford - Interviews in *The Times of India* dated 8 Dec 2003 and 6 March 2005.

Author's Profile: From Sales Executive To Sanyasi

By Kul Bhushan, the Editor

From a smartly dressed Corporate Executive in grey trousers, a blue shirt, a red tie and a tweed jacket, R Padmanabhan or Paddy as he was known, became a Sanyasi dressed in saffron-coloured cotton. The turning point came in 1986 when he was about to start a new job with a higher salary. If he had continued as a Corporate Executive, he would have probably become the Managing Director of a corporation in the ensuing 20+ years.

Presiding over a Lord Krishna dance ballet, His Divine Grace B.S. Tirtha Maharaja was seated on the stage in Navi Mumbai. One by one, local celebrities followed him on the stage, touched his feet for his blessings and sat in a semi-circle around him. They included billionaire real estate developers, senior police officers, top-level bureaucrats, judges and political leaders. On his travels to Britain, he has met Prime Ministers, ministers, members of the House of Lords and other celebrities; and has delivered discourses at Oxford and Cambridge universities. During his visits to the United

Recognition in USA

Young admirers and friends of Shrila B. S. Tirtha Maharaja, the founder Acharya of Gaudiya Vaishnava Association, pose in front of the United States Senate with a poster of the Golden Lotus Temple under construction in Navi Mumbai, India.

At a White House reception, Shrila B. S. Tirtha Maharaja is photographed with the renowned Indian industrualist Ratan Tata and Sam Pitroda, the former Information Technology advisor to the Government of India.

Shrila B.S. Tirtha Maharaja presenting Bhagavat Vani Magazine to Senator Dennis Kucinich, a former Presidential candidate, and his wife Elizabeth Jane Kucinich in Washington D.C.

At UK - US Universities

Swami B. S. Tirtha Maharaja presents the magazine of his spiritual organisation, Gaudiya Vaishnava Association, to senior members of the faculty at Georgia State University, USA.

Pictured at the Cambridge University, UK, where Swami B. S. Tirtha Maharaja delivered a discourse to the staff and students on Vedic spirituality. He has also been invited to Oxford and other leading British universities for similar talks.

After his well attended talk, Swami B. S. Tirtha Maharaja is pictured with a senior faculty member of the Washington State University, USA.

Swami B. S. Tirtha Maharaja is pictured in the campus of Maryland University in the city of College Park in Maryland, near Washington DC.

With Celebrities in UK

Swami B. S. Tirtha Maharaja meets Dhani Harrison, the son of the famous Beatle, George Harrison and talks about Krishna Consciousness and its influence on the Harrison family. Dhani is named after the 6th and 7th muscial note on the Indian scale.

During a Diwali celebration at the House of Commons, Swami B. S. Tirtha Maharaja meets the former Prime Minister of Britain Gordon Brown with the noted Aslan leader, Kelth Vaz, MP, on the left.

Swami B. S. Tirtha Maharaja greets Mr. Eric Pickles MP, Secretary of State for Communities and Local Government, Conservative Party, at the House of Commons during the Diwali celebrations.

Reaching Out with Media

Swami B. S. Tirtha Maharaja has been regulalry interviewed on radio and TV stations in US and UK and also in Australia, S. Africa and Germany, among other countries. His simple and direct answers to questions on the Vedic way of life always prompt many viewers/listners to interact with him. Here he is pictured outside the BBC studios in London.

Nathan King, Radio News Director, Georgia State University, Atlanta, USA, interviews Swami B. S. Tirtha Maharaja as this broadcast generates a great interest from listeners.

Swami B. S. Tirtha Maharaja pictured with the staff of Public Affairs Radio Station WARAS 85.5 at the University of Atlanta, USA.

States, he has been received by Senators, met mayors, chatted with congressmen, and delivered discourses in many leading universities.

Total Commitment

Would he have interacted with all these people in this manner if he had pursued his career as a Corporate Executive? At the most, he would have become the CEO or the Managing Director of a sizeable corporation to promote its products. Now he has no worldly position or titles and he promotes Krishna consciousness. Such is his total commitment to his devotion that he has all but forgotten his past life as a Corporate Executive.

A life-long celibate, he was born into a Vadagalai Iyengar Brahmin family in 1942. He learnt Sanskrit from his uncle at a very early age as he could recite up to 100 verses from a Sanskrit scripture. He passed high school and started his career in 1960 when he joined as machine operator in Indian Telephone Industries Ltd, Bangalore. He worked for about six years as a mechanic handling machines, which make winding operations for condensers and also studied part-time to become an AMIE engineer.

Not Happy

But, he was not happy with this profession. So, instead of becoming an engineer, he learned stenography and came to Bombay (now Mumbai) and got a job as a typist with Blowplast (P) Ltd in 1967. At that time, Blowplast was a private company and because of his hard work, he soon became the Personal Assistant (PA) to Mr Jal Engineeer, the Chairman and the owner of the company. As the PA to the Chairman, he worked from the office in which the Chairman was seated. Sitting next to the Chairman, he learnt the management techniques easily, because he was a participant in all activities. Many managers used to come to the Chairman for discussion and he could easily see those so-called highly educated, qualified executives trembling while talking to the Chairman. He was amazed to see their deficiencies and hollowness in spite of their high academic qualifications.

Mr Engineer used an important technique: as a manager, one should not move from one's seat. He made Paddy get the jobs done by others by telling him not to move from his seat. So he learned this technique and, surprisingly, he got a perfect response. He ensured that the required data should come to his table from all department heads. Of course, coordination was the real technique and that was very difficult to follow because sometimes it demanded persuasive charm as well as tough posture. But then, he managed and learnt the art of coordination. Later, Mr Engineer sold this company to the Piramals. Thereafter, he gradually rose in the organization, from a Depot Manager to a Branch Manager, to a Zonal Manager, on to All India Sales Manager, and finally became an Export Manager.

Well Dressed, Smart Executive

For Paddy—a well dressed, smart executive—his lifestyle was as good as any other sales executive in those days. Entertaining clients at five-star hotels, organizing dealers' conferences, regional sales conferences, all-India sales conferences, assigning sales and collection targets periodically to branch managers and field sales offices, along with other activities required to be performed by a typical sales executive of those days, were performed by him.

Promoted on Merit

He was promoted on his merit, although he had studied up to the Matric or high school. His merits included: intellectual integrity, financial honesty, loyalty, persuasive sales talk, product knowledge, a profound sense of alacrity, punctuality, pleasant manners, ability to motivate subordinates, tactfully retain all sales agencies and clients, market awareness in terms of evolving sales strategies to effectively counter the competitors' activities. On this basis he was promoted from one position to another, ultimately handling sales all over India and managing many branches for 17 years from 1967 and to 1983.

Between 1979 and 1983, he moved to Dubai, operating on an independent Trade Licence representing Blowplast. During those years, he covered the West Asia Region, part of Africa and Europe. Every month within a period of 18 days, he used to visit a minimum of six countries in the region. This meant hectic travel spending only 72 hours in each country. In 1983, there was a recession in the Middle East, and company operations handled by an independent trader without an Arab partner were becoming increasingly difficult, owing to indirect pressure from the UAE government. So, according to the management's advice from India, he wound up his operation. When Mr Manu Chabria, the owner of the well-known Jumbo Electronics in Dubai, heard that he was available, he offered him a job. He then worked for Manu Chabria from 1984 to 1986.

The Turning Point

In 1986, he went to India on a visit and got an offer from a company in the Sultanate of Oman at a much higher salary and with greater benefits. So he applied for a visa to go to Muscat.

His Divine Grace B.S. Tirtha Maharaja describes the fateful day in his own words, 'One afternoon, after a hearty lunch at a restaurant in the Flora Fountain area in Mumbai, I was walking down to take a suburban train back home. At that time I saw ISKCON devotees selling *Bhagavat Gita As It Is* by Shrila A.C. Bhaktivedanta Shrila Prabhupada, the Founder Acharya of ISKCON on a hand cart. So

I picked up one copy, came home and I finished the entire book of 700 verses of the *Gita* in less than four hours. It made me sit up.

'When I read the *Gita*, especially the second chapter, Krishna was stressing the point that you are not the body. I felt as if somebody hammered into me a few times that I was not the body. So why was I running around? Then I understood that if I am not the body, I should stop the bodily activities like my work on the material platform,' he recalls.

I am a Spirit Soul

'But as I also knew that I am a spirit soul, I was wondering what constitutes a spiritual function within this mundane world. This is explained at the end of the *Gita* in the eighteenth chapter. Its two verses explain the spiritual function very clearly:

ya idam paramam guhyam mad-bhakte hu abhidhasyati
bhaktim mayi param kritva mam evai yaty ashamshayah
(Bhagavat Gita 18.68)

'For one who explains this supreme secret to the devotees, pure devotional service is guaranteed, and at the end he will come back to Me.'

na ca tasman manushyeshu kashchin me priya-krittamah
bhavita na ca me tasmad anyah priyataro bhuvi
(Bhagavat Gita 18.69)

'There is no servant in this world more dear to Me than he, nor will there ever be one more dear.'

B.S. Tirtha Maharaja remembers, "After reading these two verses, I was convinced that this is the function of a spirit soul in the human form of life. So, when I understood this, I had formed a definite conviction and decided that this is the job I must take up from now on. From then onwards, I really thought I was wasting my time and I had wasted my time all my life up to that moment. I could imagine myself travelling to six countries a month was just like a dog jumping from one place to another. So, I stopped this jumping business and took to spreading Krishna consciousness."

Spiritual Rebirth

From this moment onwards, a genuine desire arose in his heart to devote his life to spreading the message of Krishna Consciousness by assimilating the Gaudiya Vaishnava teachings, studying the scriptures, contemplating their deeper meanings and their relevance to current situations and lifestyles. In 1989, he met his spritual master His Divine Grace Shrila Bhakti Shrirup Bhagavat Goswami Maharaj, a senior Gaudiya Vaishnava Acharya and a God-Brother of Shrila A.C. Bhaktivedanta Shrila Prabhupada, who initiated him into the Gaudiya Vaishnava tradition. Within a year in 1990, he was granted the renounced order of life (Sanyaas) by his spiritual master. He was blessed to spread everywhere, the message of Gaudiya Vaishnavism, as originated by Shri Chaitanya Mahaprabhu over five centuries ago. From 1990 to 1993, he was actively preaching in Mumbai. From 1993 to 1995, he visited Britain annually. In 1996, he toured Australia, New Zealand, Europe and the USA.

Blissful State of Affairs

Does he ever regret taking this major step moving from an executive to a Sanyasi? he is very clear, 'I was convinced thoroughly and "I had a definite conviction that Krishna is God, He is the Supreme Person, there is a spiritual world and we are basically spiritual entities, not these physical bodies. It was also clear to me that in a human form, life offers an opportunity to get back to God to serve Him with love in His abode. Because of this conviction, I never had regrets. There is no question of regretting. I had even stopped recollecting the fact that I was once a Corporate Executive. Those memories got completely obliterated without leaving a trace. I am now forced to revive my memory because of your question.

"In retrospect, I can say now that although I actively participated in those material activities from my youth till I reached the point of Krishna consciousness, I now understand that I was merely literally floating through those activities. I was never attached or attracted to those activities. Nor did any of those persons with whom I had an association and any of those relationships leave any lasting impact on me. So, although all the time, I was in a happy material situation as well, the blissful state of affairs that I am now going through is no comparison to it at *all*."

B.S. Tirtha Maharaja concludes, "I can confidently say that this can be tried by mundane worker of this modern day. One should not waste his time, but start on the spiritual task of spreading Krishna consciousness all over the world and awaken the sleeping souls. One should impress upon the general masses their eternal relationship with God Krishna to attain complete tranquillity while being here in this world. This will also enable one to gain an eternal residence in the transcendental realm of Goloka Vrindavana for rendering loving service to the Supreme Divine Couple, Radha-Krishna. Hare Krishna!"

Editor's Profile: Kul Bhushan

The Author and the Editor

A journalist, an editor, an author, a publisher and a media consultant, Kul Bhushan has worked at senior levels in different countries and continents for over 40 years with international and multi-national organizations. After starting to write for newspapers in Kenya in 1950s, he passed with honours a course in Advanced Journalism at the Nairobi University conducted by the International Press Institute in 1966.

A year later, he joined the biggest newspaper group in East Africa, The Nation as a Senior Correspondent and later, appointed as the first Business Editor in Kenya. He moved to another leading newspaper, 'The Standard' as the Economics Editor.

He was invited to the World Bank/IMF headquarters to interview its then President, Tom Clausen and honoured with the Journalist of the Year Award by the Kenyan President Moi. He resigned after working as a full time editor for 22 years. During this period, he was also the East African Correspondent for AIR, PTI and UNI. In 2005, he started a weekly column on NRIs for IANS.

He has written 26 books including a reference book on Kenya that ran into 16 editions to become the authoritative business and economic reference book. In 2005, he wrote HOW TO DEAL WITH VAT with a Foreword by the then Finance Minister P. Chidambaram published by Pearson that became a bestseller. He established his publishing company in Nairobi in 1970 to publish the Kenya reference book, magazines and newsletters. In 1988, he established Newstech Publishing Inc in New Delhi, www.newstechglobal.com

As a member of the International Press Institute, the global body of editors and publishers, he represented this organisation in Africa for seven years and edited their Pan-African Economic Development News Service. In 1997, he became a Media Consultant to the United Nations Industrial Development Organization (UNIDO) at its headquarters in Vienna, Austria, for three years and later, for the UNIDO Regional Office in New Delhi.

Always been attracted to spirituality, he interviewed many leading Indian gurus and visited the holy places of many religions in different countries. Over 30 years ago, he was initiated by an enlightened spiritual master. Since then, reading spiritual literature, listening to spiritual masters and meditating are an important part of his life. With his travels to over 50 countries, his experience with a UN organisation, he brings a global and a positive perspective to his writing.

Kul Bhushan

kb@kulbhushan.net

।। श्री श्री गुरू गौरांगौ जयतः ।।

Love God, Not Fear Him

GAUDA is the sacred land in India between the Himalayan Mountains and the north of the Vindhya Hills. Called Gauda Desh or Gauda Country, it was also known as Aryavarta or the Land of the Aryas. It covers Kashmir, Punjab, Uttar Pradesh, Madhya Pradesh, Bihar and Bengal. Later, Bengal became popular as Gauda Desh.

VAISHNAVA means 'Related to Vishnu' - the Supreme Lord. The original source of Lord Vishnu is Lord Krishna, Who says in the Gita that all living beings are part of Him. Hence everyone, as a soul, is basically a Vaishnava. The Vaishnavas accept that Lord Vishnu/Lord Krishna is the Supreme Person.

GAUDIYA VAISHNAVISM. The Gaudiya Vaishnavas believe that one should love God and not fear Him. Since the lover and the beloved must possess a form to give and receive love, the Gaudiya Vaishnavas worship Lord Krishna Who has all transcendental attributes of Godhood. The Gaudiya Vaishnavas thus display the highest levels of this loving relationship. Chaitanya Mahaprabhu, non-different from Krishna, is the supreme role model for all devotees, Who laid the foundation of Gaudiya Vaishnavism over five centuries ago in Bengal. Through the chanting of the Holy Names of Lord Krishna, He distributed transcendental love and unfolded the secret for entering into the highest eternal loving relationship with the Supreme Lord, Sri Krishna.

Gaudiya Vaishnava Association (GVA)

Is a spiritual congregation striving to enlighten everyone about the most important goal of life - Krishna Consciousness or unconditional love and devotion to Lord Krishna, the Supreme Personality of Godhead. GVA's sole aim is to promote peace and harmony by spreading spiritual knowledge and remove the misery caused by hankering for material gains in today's materialistic world. Under the spiritual guidance of Shrila B. S. Tirtha Maharaj, GVA welcomes everyone, without any distinction, to take part in its activities such as prayer meetings, sankirtans, cultural activities and private discussions. Daily Bhagavad Gita classes and weekly feast programmes are held at the GVA Temples in Navi Mumbai and Kolkata. Other GVA Centres are in New Delhi, London, UK; Atlanta, USA; and Sydney, Australia.

।। श्री श्री गुरू गौरांगौ जयतः ।।

GVA Philosophy

The Philosophy

- The Vedic Knowledge received through an authoritative line of spiritual teachers is the perfect transcendental knowledge.
- The Supreme Lord Sri Hari is the Supreme Truth.
- He possesses innumerable potencies.
- He is the nectarine ocean of all rasas, the transcendental mellows.
- Living entities, souls (jivas) are His fragmentary portions.
- Certain entities are captivated by Maya, the illusory potency of Sri Hari.
- Some of them eternally stay free from it.
- All potencies (Spiritual, Marginal and Material) are inconceivably simultaneously one with, and different from, Sri Hari.
- Pure unalloyed devotional service is the only process.

- Unalloyed spontaneous affection for Sri Hari is the ultimate objective to be accomplished.

The Objectives

- To spread spiritual awareness all over the world.
- To make people realise the futility of mere material advancement devoid of God consciousness.
- To impress upon the people's minds, the usefulness of stratification (Daiva Varnashrama system) of human society according to the Vedic system aimed at ultimate spiritual perfection.
- To assist the ignorant suffering masses to understand the actual goal of human life, i. e. to re-establish the lost relationship with God.
- To propagate, preach and promote the only means of deliverance — the chanting of the Holy Names of God - Sri Krishna.

।। श्री श्री गुरू गौरांगौ जयतः ।।

GVA Way of Life

FOOD: Vegetarian—but merely becoming vegetarian is not enough.

The food should be procured by committing the least violence. According to the 'Gita', it should be 'Sattvik'. The food must first be offered to Lord Krishna and Radha Rani and then be accepted as 'Prasadam' or blessed food.

EDUCATION: Should not be merely for economic development and gain of power but more for evolving into a better human being with highly pure moral character, who observes and appreciates the Lord's beauty and potency in everything that be, ever ready to serve Lord Krishna with everything he possesses.

SPIRITUALITY: Chanting Hare Krishna Maha Mantra at every opportunity instantly purifies the minds of both the chanter and the hearer. Thus audibly chanting Hare Krishna Maha Mantra on beads (japa) for a specific number of rounds daily is a must because this transcendental vibration helps one control the mind, makes the environment auspicious and makes all the evils flee.

CAREER: Working honestly and with optimum or 'samyak' effort without hankering for reward as given in the Gita. Avoiding interaction with gross materialists and atheists, even if they are close relatives, friends or colleagues as they hinder progress in Krishna Consciousness.

MARRIAGE: Being faithful and committed to married life as given in the scriptures.

।। श्री श्री गुरू गौरांगौ जयतः ।।

Gaudiya Vaishnava Tradition

Lord Sri Krishna, the Supreme Personality – the source of all creation, spiritual and material. He is the one and only God for all life-forms thriving within His creation. He alone is the fulfiller of all their wishes and all good qualities seen in them are nothing but infinitesimally small manifestations of His own superlative traits.

Lord Sri Chaitanya Mahaprabhu, the most munificent of all incarnations of Lord Sri Krishna. He is none other than Sri Krishna imbued with the highest loving sentiments of His dearest consort, Srimati Radharani. He is the Hero of all those who find love in the chanting of the Holy Names of Sri Sri Radha Krishna and the only refuge for those who desperately long for winning their servanthood.

His Divine Grace Bhaktisiddhanta Saraswati Goswami Thakura, Jagatguru Srila Prabhupada – the powerhouse of Lord Sri Chaitanya Mahaprabhu's preaching movement. He single-handedly revived and re-established Gaudiya Vaishnavism in the highly corrupt, lustful and atheistic society of today's world and is worshipped by all existing Gaudiya Vaishnava Acharyas as their Spiritual Master.

His Divine Grace Bhakti Srirupa Bhagavat Goswami Maharaj, one of the dearest disciples of Jagatguru Srila Prabhupada. He was one of the greatest exponents of the Srimad Bhagavatam and a loving devotion. He earnestly preached the philosophy and distributed the love of Sri Chaitanya Mahaprabhu among the ignorant and suffering masses to free them from the vicious cycle of birth and death till the very last day of his stay in this material world.

His Divine Grace Bhaktivedanta Shrila Prabhupad, another favourite and outstanding disciple of Jagatguru Srila Prabhupada. He is most famous as the Founder Acharya of ISKCON and one of the most powerful preachers of Lord Sri Chaitanya Mahaprabhu's Bhakti Movement to have ever walked the earth. Due to his indefatigable and painstaking efforts that today Sri Chaitanya Mahaprabhu is known and worshipped in nearly all the major towns of the world.

His Divine Grace Shrila B.S. Tirtha Maharaj, the most ardent disciple of His Divine Grace Bhakti Srirupa Bhagavat Goswami Maharaj and Founder Acharya of the GVA. One of the most philosophically perfect, astoundingly knowledgeable, unbelievably humble and exceptionally dignified Gaudiya Vaishnava Acharyas of modern times. His humility and loving devotion can make the most hard-hearted atheist fall at his feet and his knowledge and lucid explanations can win the heart of the most obstinate and conceited scientist.

।। श्री श्री गुरू गौरांगौ जयतः ।।

GVA Global Contacts

GVA PRINCIPAL CENTRE
Mumbai, India
Gaudiya Vaishnava Association
Parsik Hill, Uran Road, Belapur
Navi Mumbai 400 614, India
Tel: +91 842 090 4322
email: dasa.gauranga108@gmail.com

GVA – Kolkata, India
Gaudiya Vaishnava Association
BhajanKutir, P-74 CIT,
Scheme VII M, Kankurgachi
Kolkata – 700 054, India
Tel: - +91 842 090 4322
email: dasa.gauranga108@gmail.com

GVA – Atlanta, USA
Gaudiya Vaishnava Association
4795, Morton Bridge Lane
Alpharetta, Georgia 30022
USA
Tel: 1-888-9-GVA-USA (1-888-948-2872)
Email: usa@bhagavatvani.org
www.bhagavatvani.org

Gaur Govinda Trust – London, UK
22 Cromwell Road
Wembley,
HA0 IJS, UK
Tel: +44 (0)7877 404 733
email: gaurgovindatrust@gmail.com
www.gaurgovindatrust.org

Gaur Govinda Centre Inc. – Australia
80 Stuart Road, Dharruk
New South Wales 2770
Australia
Tel: +61 (0) 426 811 160
email: savyasacidas@bhagavatvani.org

"Mirror, Mirror on the wall,

who is the unhappiest of all?"

The problem today is that nine out of ten times,the mirror will point at you!

Yes, you.It could be that despite your best efforts you never get the results or the rewards you expect. Or, having made it to the top with all the comforts and luxuries, you are always worried, stressed and tense.

If you are struggling for the good life and not getting anywhere, you need a different frame of mind to survive.

If you are 'a success' in terms of this world and are still unhappy, then you need to know that with every material gain that gives you happiness, also attached is unhappiness. Despite these problems, you could make your life worth living by expressing your love and devotion to Sri Krishna by chanting His Holy Names and thus rising above the battle against worldly attractions or the mirage of Maya. This is done by taking part in 'Sankirtana' in the company of like-minded devotees of Lord Krishna.

The Gaudiya Vaishnava Association provides a venue for all the people of the world to come together to offer their total devotion to Lord Krishna in 'Sankirtan'. Then you rise above or go beyond material duality of failure and success, happiness and unhappiness. And you need not ask the mirror any questions!